CW00518419

Wacky

"J'ai rêvé dans la grotte où nage la sirène."
Gèrard de Nerval

Hey diddle, diddle,
He clings to the middle
Of a broomstick aloft in the skies.
The little cat howls as he loses his hold
And falls to an earthly demise

But sealed is his Fate
For he has a date,
One nurtured by gods for a hero
Re-born of the foam, he will find a new home
A Ship's Cat he is destined to be-o!

Wacky

The Diary of a Ship's Cat

The True Story of a Ship's Cat's Adventures
From Hellas to the Hebrides

written by himself

enabled by his pet, Zanthoula
aka Ursula Haselden

illustrated by Gill Waugh

Seashell

Copyright © Ursula Haselden 2016
Illustrations copyright © Gill Waugh
First published in 2016 by Seashell
Lechine House, Lochearnhead, Perthshire, FK19 8PY

Distributed by Gardners Books, 1 Whittle Drive, Eastbourne,
East Sussex, BN23 6QH
Tel: +44(0)1323 521555 | Fax: +44(0)1323 521666

British Library Cataloguing in Publication Data
A catalogue record for this book is available from the British Library.

ISBN 978-0-9556291-1-2

Typeset by Amolibros, Milverton, Somerset
www.amolibros.com
This book production has been managed by Amolibros
Printed and bound by T J International Ltd, Padstow, Cornwall, UK

Wacky's Diary

Acknowledgements

I would like to express my thanks to Zanthoula for enabling the publication of this diary and to the Captain of *Cappelle* for his forbearance with an unruly kitten, for teaching me games and for passing on the navigational skills necessary to my profession. I am grateful too for his proofreading of my paw-written manuscript, subsequently lovingly scrutinised by Jane Tatam of Amolibros, my publishing consultant. All the many friends, human, feline, canine and veterinary, who played a formative part in my life, are remembered with pleasure and gratitude. This includes Gaby Gauthier, aged nine, to whom I taught English and who, in turn, polished my French, Korina Tsimpos of Thessaloniki, who caught fish for me, my buddy Socky, my boon companion on Lesbos, and little Jo-Jo of Beirut ("Woof! Woof!") in Cyprus. I am truly flattered that the National Cat Club of Great Britain should invite me to make a celebrity appearance at their Exhibition at Olympia.

I wish also to remember the late, great Hamish McHamish of St Andrews, who introduced me to the Old Grey Toon. I am indebted to Mairi Hedderwick, the "Lady Artist", for permitting me to spend a day with my pen friend Fabbydou on the island of Coll, and I have been truly blessed by my illustrator, Gill Allan Waugh of Balquhidder, who, despite illness, completed her drawings of me from contemporary photographs. I am indebted also to Richard Unthank, who expertly mapped the twists and turns of my unforgettable voyage.

The quotation on page 211 is from the musical *Lady in the Dark* with lyrics by Ira Gershwin.

This diary is dedicated to all sailors, cat lovers and feral cats everywhere.

27 February 2016

Able-bodied Seaman
"WACKY"
Ship's Cat
c/o S/Y CAPPELLE
Yacht-in-Transit

Contents

Maps		x-xi
Prelude		xiii
ONE	Artemis and Wacky	1
TWO	Tribulations and a New Collar	10
THREE	My First Christmas and a Rite of Passage	14
FOUR	Graduation	21
FIVE	Danger	26
SIX	A Greeting from the Red Arrows	31
SEVEN	Heavy Weather	35
EIGHT	A Hilarious Dinner Party	39
NINE	A Night Sail in Tandem	44
TEN	My New Friend	49
ELEVEN	A Leap for Salvation	58
TWELVE	Islanders Friendly and Unfriendly	62
THIRTEEN	The Forbidden Republic	66
FOURTEEN	Land Base with Resident Witch	72
FIFTEEN	Landfall in Turkey	78
SIXTEEN	The Central Islands	84
SEVENTEEN	Land of Peel Towers	90
EIGHTEEN	I Salute an Icon and Exit Greek Waters	95
NINETEEN	Landfall in Italy	101
TWENTY	Wacky and Odysseus	105

TWENTY-ONE	Mugged in the Aeolians	112
TWENTY-TWO	Stromboli	117
TWENTY-THREE	Corsican Interlude	122
TWENTY-FOUR	Odysseus Again	126
TWENTY-FIVE	We Cross to France	131
TWENTY-SIX	A Shadow Overhangs	137
TWENTY-SEVEN	I Leave Solo on a Big Adventure	143
TWENTY-EIGHT	Riverbanking	151
TWENTY-NINE	We Sail the South Coast	158
THIRTY	An English Christmas	161
THIRTY-ONE	East Coast Interlude	167
THIRTY-TWO	West Coast of Scotland	171
THIRTY-THREE	A Cat of Distinction	176
THIRTY-FOUR	The Corryvrechan	181
THIRTY-FIVE	A Friendship is Cemented	185
THIRTY-SIX	We Move Berth	191
THIRTY-SEVEN	Extrasensory Perception	194
THIRTY-EIGHT	Tir-na-nOg	198

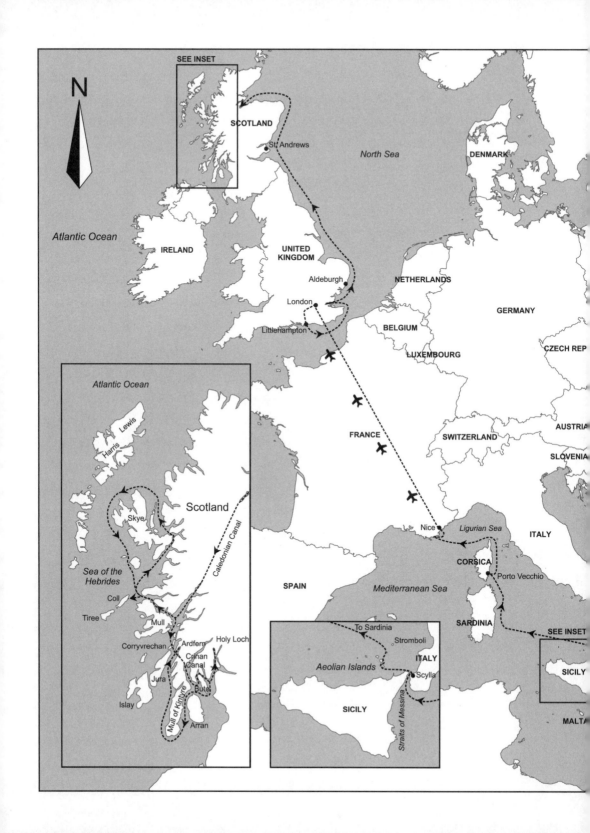

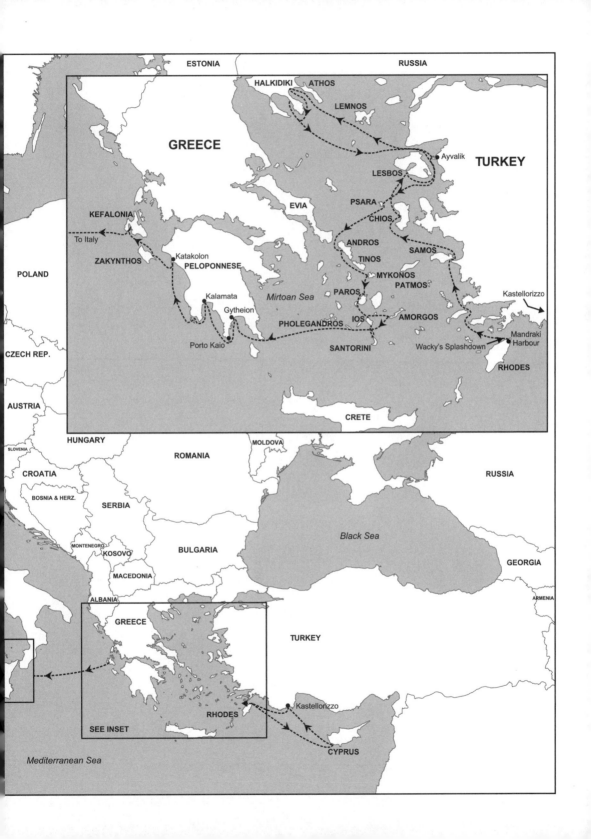

Prelude

I declare this diary to be a true record of the odyssey undertaken by me as Ship's Cat on a small British sailing yacht, S/Y *Cappelle*, on her voyage from Hellas to the Northern Isles, in other words from the Aegean Islands, into which I was unwittingly cast, to those of the far Hebrides.

This introduction is necessary, so that you may understand the singular nature of my beginnings. My diary was not presented to me until the New Year's Day succeeding my mysterious arrival in the sea off Rhodes. By then I was some three months old, had done a little growing up (but not all) and had settled into my new home, *Cappelle*, a thirty-four-foot wooden sloop flying the Red Ensign.

Before starting the first page of my pristine diary, I was coached in the rudiments of paw writing by the Captain. It was evident I was of Greek origin and that I was already well versed in the classics.

ONE

Artemis and Wacky

In which I fall from a broomstick.

My splashdown, rescue and recuperation on S/Y *Cappelle*.

I spread fleas and gain a name.

My arrival on earth is a blur. All I remember is riding pillion on the broomstick of the goddess Artemis who, as everyone knows, created the cat. I was the latest addition to her brood. The broomstick acted like a launch pad. All of a sudden the stars were turning somersaults and I was tumbling through space to land with a horrendous splash in breaking wavelets.

I had descended to earth beside sea-shuffled rocks, which is why they call me "born of the foam" (just like Aphrodite, they say). My landing was very near the spot where the Colossus of Rhodes, a giant statue of the Sun God, planted his right foot. Until destroyed by earthquake, this statue straddled the entrance to what was to become Mandraki Yacht Harbour on the island of Rhodes.

Was it an accident? Did I fall or was I pushed? It's hard to say. I have this sneaky suspicion it was meant to be. That Artemis had a mission for me. (She was known to be pretty ruthless with her offspring.) Perhaps she noticed the yellow flecks in my eyes, a sign of natural-born sorcery? But at birth into this world I was only a little black-and-white malkin with great big paws, a warm heart and an oddly bent ear.

"All I remember is riding pillion on the broomstick of the goddess Artemis who, as everyone knows, created the cat."

Wet, cold and very, very scared, not surprisingly I did the only thing I knew how and yelled my head off every time it bobbed up out of the nasty, cold, salt water as I struggled, gasping for air. If each howl were to be my last, it was going to be the most far-reaching I could muster. The world was going to know about me! And my predicament.

How I longed for Artemis to come back! I know, in the heavens, I had only been a wriggly kitten, squirming on her broomstick, instead of providing due support for her night sight (my kind has excellent night sight, while that of the gods and goddesses is notoriously deficient), but I did not deserve to be treated so. "*Dum spiro, spero!*" "While I breathe, I hope!" I thought desperately. If the last thing I ever did was to speak my mind, it was going to be LOUD! Then I recollected a terrible Greek swearword – it's amazing the language you can pick up while travelling through space. I won't tell you what the swearword was, but it began with "*Μάλακα...!*", which is dreadfully bad and certainly not for kittens.

It wasn't my goddess mother who heard me – Artemis must have been away over the horizon long ago – but Zanthoula, which, in Greek, means small blonde person. She was a human bean. The noise I made grated on her ears and set her teeth on edge as she stood doing the washing-up in the galley of the boat I was to come to know so well. Turning the radio off to listen, she concluded – such was the persistence of my high-pitched screeching – I must be a hungry seagull, a human baby bean throwing a spectacular tantrum or even a power tool wielded by a boat person – boat people can be notoriously inconsiderate about disturbing other people, even on a Sunday morning. Then she gathered up her shopping bag and climbed ashore to get away from the noise. (When the going gets tough, girls go shopping.)

Once on the quay, the pitch was even louder and Zanthoula, realising that something, or someone, had a problem, knew she must investigate. Homing in on the noise, she crossed to the Old Fort of St Nicholas on the end of the harbour mole, reckoning she might have to climb because whatever-it-was was stuck high up on the mediaeval walling. But when she glanced down at her feet she saw ME, barging about in the waves, colliding with the rocks below. She was really quite rude when first she addressed me: "You're not very pretty, are you?" she said. (What a thing to say to anyone in extremis!) To be frank, I didn't give a scallop shell about not being pretty. But I did want to be rescued.

Was I a sorry sight? I was filthy, fishy and clotted with tar. I know Zanthoula meant well, but what she did was to drop me, flotsam that I was – hypothermic, dripping wet and sticky – into her shopping bag. To add to my troubles, I then found myself suffocated in a wicker basket. I could hear passing tourists remonstrating with her – what did they know? – as she hurried along clutching a squalling shopping bag.

"Don't worry! I've got a kitten. I DON'T WANT TO KEEP IT!" (famous last words) she said to the man who came to meet her. (I wasn't an "it" I was ME!, I thought furiously.) "I just want to clean it up and let it go with the feral cat colony!" Through a slit in the basketwork, I could see she was addressing a tall human bean, who looked a proper καπετάνιος, a boat captain.

The precious receptacle, with me in it, was handed over. We climbed a rail and descended a short flight of steps. It was cool and shady down there, but the floor swayed alarmingly, reminding me of the wobbly broomstick. Then Zanthoula lifted me out and put me on newspaper. My trouble was I simply could not stop screeching! It was as if my vocal mechanism was so wound up it refused to run down. Zanthoula proceeded to smear Marmite (disgusting stuff) on the end of my nose – to divert my attention, she told the Captain. (I have not thought much of Marmite since.) "Let the gods be kind!" I prayed, as she set about rubbing me down with a rough towel, which made my fur come out in tufts, before using cotton buds to poke stuff out of my eyes and ears and nostrils. All the while she rabbited on about how ill-favoured I was – great big spoon feet, a badly deformed ear and all the rest. Not a kitten fit for adoption. Anyway, I wouldn't chose a black-and-white one, she said. Not words to give confidence. How insulting! How could she! You'd think she might have been more tactful! I know my myopic eyes were bleary. But did she not notice the yellow flecks for spice? I admit I was only a half-drowned kitty with a cabbage ear. But I tried to tell her I was SPECIAL, that I was born of the gods and that Artemis would be looking for me – so WATCH IT! All Zanthoula did in reply was to give me pappy stuff called bread-and-milk, hardly manna from the gods. I wouldn't touch it. I demanded mother's milk.

Zanthoula could see I was poorly, so she let me follow my instinct, which was to crawl away to hide and fall asleep and die and go to paradise. The safe house I chose for my projected demise was the darkest, most malodorous corner I could find, the damp corner under the outlet pipe behind the loo, a Baby Blake of the sort, they say, that has broken up many a budding romance between a human bean boy and girl. This location suited my mood and condition, and here I cried convulsively all day long.

By evening I was in a bad way, spewing lungfuls of sea water and retching so piteously that my new mother (I was beginning to recognise Zanthoula for what she was) was concerned about me. Dragging me out from my insalubrious sanctuary, she laid me on a towel at the foot of her berth so that she could put out a comforting hand in the night. But I refused to settle. Waving my small, stiff tail for balance, I staggered up her outstretched form as she lay in bed until I could push my face into the warm spot round the back of her neck underneath her long hair, in a nesting sort of way, convinced that somewhere about her person, if only I could find it, lay a teat full of warm mother's milk. I decided the teat, if not round the back of her neck, must be inside her ear, so I pushed my nose down it, sucking and kneading with oversized paws. Sometimes I dropped into an exhausted sleep, only to jerk awake with nightmare visions and hunger pangs and start the cycle over. It was the most unquiet night either of us ever spent.

My Pets had purchased tickets for the early bus to Lindos that day. Seeing I was still (albeit reluctantly) alive, Zanthoula furnished me with every convenience before they left. There was a place on her warm patch, a baking tray filled with beach gravel for my toilet and a bowl of fresh water. In the event, with me in mind, my Pets cut their trip short and came home sooner than expected.

Consternation! In the cabin silence reigned. Where could I be? How could the orphan have got out? There were dark patches on the cushions and spittle on the carpet, proof that I had been retching up seawater. But no sign of me. Then a faint hiss alerted Zanthoula to another damp corner, the far recesses of the black hole under the draining board behind the sink pipe. Thrusting her arm into the edgy darkness she touched fur and dragged me out, a pitiable little object foaming at the mouth and doing its best to spit. (In an effort to defend myself I put on my best Tasmanian Devil act to prove I was not a Child of Artemis for nothing.) *"Ψιψινάκι μου!"* ("My little pussy cat!") Zanthoula cooed in Greek, ignoring my fury, but overjoyed to find me alive.

Within twenty minutes, though my stomach heaved and I retched, my frantic heart beats slowed and I began to cheer up. Maybe there was more to life after all? There followed comforting bouts of deep, refreshing sleep. Soon I was ready to try drinking out of my new blue bowl, although at first I couldn't work out how to get my tongue in the water without putting my nose in first. By the third day I was nibbling scraps, experimenting with my dirt tray and squeezing behind the spare water tank in the forepeak (another dark sequestered spot).

I grew cheeky.

I developed a penchant for chewing bare toes and suckling on skin. The only action that drove me crazy was any attempt to take me off the boat. As far as I was concerned it was home and I intended to stay on it, safe and sound, for ever and ever.

A lovely human bean called Mireille, who was French and one of Zanthoula's boat friends, dropped by to meet me. Regarding me thoughtfully, she said, *"Il a senti le beau bateau."* I had cried and cried until taken aboard, she surmised. (It must be explained that cats understand ALL languages right across the globe – whereas human beans, on the other hand, often have difficulty in working out the proper meaning of even a well-spoken "Meow!" – which only goes to show!) I

Wet, cold and very very scared...

at once understood what *Κυρία* Mireille meant. She was right – I had sensed the presence of the beautiful boat while tumbling through the skies, subliminally registering it as my destiny.

Someone produced a book on cat astrology. I was reckoned to be four to five weeks old, which meant I had been born under the sign of Leo, a lucky sign. But the question of a name remained outstanding. ("A cat needs a name that's particular," said Mark Twain.) A name endows power and should be expressive of personality. "Mandraki", after the yacht harbour, was mooted, but this failed to stick, which meant it was the wrong name. "Colossus" would have suited better because of where I pitched up and, let's face it, my big feet. But then along came Julia, another friend of Zanthoula, who declared I reminded her of Pyewacket, the familiar spirit in *Bell, Book and Candle*. "Born-of-the-gods, he's a witch's cat!", declared Julia. She was right! Thus, combined with my particular distinction of a deformed ear, I became "Wacky", a name that was truly mine. Mireille spoke of my aural disfigurement as *"sa marque"* ("his mark") believing it akin to the lightning-bolt on Harry Potter's forehead. It was my badge of honour. It set me apart. It was even, dare it be whispered, a sign of future greatness! (When, many years later, I was invited to take a ride across the famous Harry Potter viaduct on the original Hogwart's Express, I remembered Julia's remark.)

Alas, my physical appearance failed to improve along with my sense of well-being. On noticing fleas running through my fur, Zanthoula put on her hat (not something she normally did of an evening) and made for the nearest pharmacy. (I say "put on her hat" advisedly. Around the period of my "accident", and connected with the strangely turbulent skies of the time, my Pets suffered a rough passage from Turkey to the Greek island of Rhodes, leading to a nasty black eye for Zanthoula.) What a pretty pair we made! For a while Zanthoula felt more acceptable angling her trilby hat of Dedham straw over her bad eye when facing the public.

Zanthoula's visit to the pharmacy was a singular humiliation. Far from being deceived by her nattily tipped titfer, the pharmacist's assistant found her appearance tellingly dissolute – especially when she asked for flea powder. (You never knew with boat people!) Although Zanthoula was at pains to explain she was buying the flea powder on behalf of a cat, it was obvious the assistant did not believe her. Looking down her nose, she backed off to push a puff-pack of "Pubex" in Zanthoula's direction at the end of a long ruler. (Who would waste money on a cat anyway? Everyone knows they are vermin!)

TWO

Tribulations and a New Collar

In which my fur falls out.

Zanthoula and I develop Ring Worm.

I take to a collar, but refuse to step on terra firma.

It is autumn and these are our halcyon days. Dawn brings Bluebirds of Happiness. Low, swift and direct in flight, emitting piercing whistles, they populate the harbour more numerously than boats, sharing our world but not of it. Compact, short-necked and rapier-beaked, preening on cap rails they scan the water to pinpoint a fish before making a sudden dart. A jeweller's delight, as solid and scintillating as Fabergé eggs, kingfishers swing on anchor chains in the early sun, catching fire in ruby, sapphire, green and gold. I develop quite an attachment to one little feller. I am only a youngster myself, so he knows he has nothing to fear when we share *Cappelle's* stern deck.

In looks I remain far from prepossessing – as people never fail to point out. After the fleas flee, my fur comes out in handfuls. Bare in patches and scabby-nosed, I am greeted with, "Hi there! Scruffy!" I find myself whispered about as the "Ugly Kitling". Artemis would be disgusted with the state of my person. But she no longer seems to care.

Oh woe is me and lack-a-day! Things are to become considerably worse. On developing scarlet lesions on her chest where I like to lay my head, Zanthoula takes to swimming in a shirt. Her affliction spreads rapidly.

When the itchy red rosettes appear on her arms and neck, she puts on long sleeves, knowing there is only one thing for it. She will have to brave a further visit to the pharmacy The assistant does not prevaricate but, blurting out "Γιατρό!" ("Doctor!"), shows her the door.

Greek doctors specialise. Zanthoula knows she must seek a dermatologist. When she sets off, wan-faced, to walk to her appointment at a surgery in the suburbs, she twice loses her way in fear of arrival. What concerns her is not so much herself, but that she will be advised to get rid of me and neither of us are prepared for that! However, white-coated Dr Koutalianos greets her kindly and, when on looking at her lesions says, "You are English! I think you have a cat! Don't worry! This is not a problem! It happens all the time. In England you call it 'Ring Worm'. Correctly, it is a fungus that is easily cured." Seeing my Pet so upset, he reads her thoughts and goes on gently. "And would you like me to treat your cat as well, for I think you wish to keep him. It is best I treat you both together." Zanthoula left with a spring in her step, prescriptions for us both and a glowing opinion of Greek doctors.

We recover fast. My fur grows thick and lustrous and Zanthoula's skin regains its glow. She is back in her bikini in no time. And I feel so well and confident that I set about exploring my new domain. There is another damp cave in the forepeak, called the anchor locker, with which I acquaint myself but now feel no desire to hide in. I have better things to do. Life holds promise.

The Captain makes me toys. Among my favourite playthings are a cardboard loo-roll with a crackly foil bottle top sellotaped inside and a float on a piece of string fastened to a locker handle. There is cat's cradle too with the strings of sleeping bags. This is a game I often practise as I lie on my back somewhere nice and soft until I fell asleep.

It could be said that I wanted for nothing. The Captain even remarks (a little ruefully perhaps, for not all Captains would put up with it) that the cabin resembles a nursery. There is always fresh water for me to drink and a dirt tray, with proper cat litter purchased by Zanthoula, is provided. Moreover there is always something tasty in my blue bowl on the shelf below the cooker. Whenever the bowl is empty I sit beside it wearing my most appealing expression until Zanthoula fills it up again.

The boss says I am as clever as chop-sticks. I notice when Zanthoula changes the colour of her head-band. When she put on her sun hat to go shopping, I take to my bed to await her return. It is the Captain who teaches me my best games. He is brilliant at this. He is also my coach in turning back somersaults off his knee, at which I became adept, frequently demonstrating my acrobatic skills just to show off. I also do tricks when I want something badly but nobody has noticed. It makes my Pets sit up all right! The most riotous game of all is when the Captain nets me in a bundle of string tied with enough toys to render me a feline one-man band. I can hardly wait to go into my Houdini act, extricating myself so fast they can't believe their eyes when the clinking whirligig turned into ME, standing there breathless, ever eager to be tied up again.

But *terra firma* remains strictly *non grata*. (As you will notice, being born a classicist, I am familiar with Latin.) When well-meaning boat live-aboard neighbours fashion a gang-plank to encourage me ashore, I eschew all their attempts to persuade me down it. Not even cajoling words and a juicy fish dangled at the bottom cut any ice with me. My short experience of *terra firma* has not been good, and that, I decide, is that. I am better off on the boat Artemis chose for me.

Zanthoula thinks of everything. She has the shoemaker cut me a red leather puppy collar to size and hangs on it an Evil Eye, a φυλαχτό (amulet) for my protection. I don't need persuading to wear such a collar. In fact I am soon unhappy without it! Adopting the badge of a proper Ship's Cat boosts my self-esteem. The collar is smart too. The sight of me wearing such an attractive accessory reduces poor French boat-wife, Denise, to tears. Denise has never recovered from the loss of her own Ship's Cat, Zéus, "*si beau, si gracieux*" and still hopes against hope for his return. But he has been missing for a month and it looks as if he never will come back. (I would like to meet Zéus. With a name like that we might have much in common. I expect he is off somewhere on the business of the gods.)

Then *Buckingham Palace*, a large Australian motor-sailer, puts in with Sam aboard. Sam is a Siamese-if-you-please, friendly, but a dreamy soul, a nose-in-the-air nut case you might say, a description that arises from the fact that he once tried to walk down his own gangplank when it wasn't there. Not noticing the plank had been removed for cleaning, Sam, not surprisingly, did a vertical plunge into harbour. Though he was fished out spluttering, it made a big dent in his amour propre. Sam was furnished with a posh loo, a sort of Palace of Convenience. The opportunity for promotion this afforded me is too good to miss and I take to jumping across to *Buckingham Palace* to share it. Once I called on Sam to come out to play at two o'clock in the morning, but he was fast asleep with his Pets and I got sent home with a flea in my ear. (Well, it was worth a try!)

And once I jumped aboard *Buckingham Palace* just as, unbeknownst to me, she was about to move berth. When some hostile bean attempted to grab me, I fought like crazy, tooth and nail, as the saying goes, on the assumption I was being kidnapped. In the end I was reunited with my Pets wrapped in a thick blanket by a man wearing leather gauntlets. (I hope that taught that *Buckingham Palace* lot a lesson, and I suppose I learnt one too.)

This is the beginning of my leaving my boat for short intervals by hopping from side-deck to side-deck. (I still refused to step on terra firma.) There was never any question of my quitting for good. As Mireille said of my kind, "Ils s'attachent." And when we do, that's it, for life.

THREE

My First Christmas and a Rite of Passage

In which we celebrate Christmas.

I help teach a French boy English.

The sap rises and I suffer a rite of passage.

At a special festival time called Christmas, Zanthoula assumes official charge of *Cappelle*, while the Captain, assigning me the duties of Chief Mate, goes to London. Zanthoula buys stick-on silver stars for the cabin walls, ties her hair with red tinsel and winds more tinsel round my collar, so we both display Christmas cheer. We get lots of invitations. (Actually it is Zanthoula who gets the invitations, but I accompany her as her Familiar and Guard Cat, whether invited or not.)

The Town Council broadcasts a seasonal cassette, "White Christmas" in Greek. Amplified and endlessly reiterated, it becomes an ear-plugging bore. Worse is the poisoned meat thrown onto the quay from a Council van to cull the feral cat population. Thank goodness I stayed home, but I do lose some friends, including Gateau, a pretty tortoiseshell, beloved of a little German girl, who tragically got caught up in the extermination programme. Gateau, of course, not the German girl.

The Captain returns from London loaded with presents, including cat toys and cat treats. He also brings more Famous Five books for Gaby, Mireille's nine-year-old son, whom Zanthoula is teaching English. Gaby spends two hours every day, except Sunday, with us. He now has a new baby brother, Simon, on his boat, so it is nice for him to be independent. He loves the Enid Blyton adventure stories. On his arrival in the morning we first play a rattling good game of cabin tag and then have a snack to set us up, before, armed with his *cahier* (exercise book), Gaby gets down to work on the cabin table, with me sitting beside him to breathe encouragement. (The good news is that Gaby soon grows so fluent in English that, not long after we leave Rhodes, he wins a part in an American film being shot on the island. What is more he is presented with the splendid new racing bike he rides in the film. So you can say I helped launch a film star! (Hooray for me!)

"Και του χρόνου!" ("Here's to next year!") is what we Greeks say as a New Year greeting. When Zanthoula wakes up in pouring rain on New Year's Day she writes on the first page of the new diary the Captain gives her, that contentment is "a duvet, a cat, a hot-water bottle, a good book, a cup of tea and melted Mars bar to eat with a spoon." (At least I feature almost top of the list!)

The day is significant, for the Captain has a New Year gift for me too, a beautiful book. Tooled on its pristine cover in splendid gold lettering is the name

WACKY

Underneath are the words:

THE DIARY OF A SHIP'S CAT

The fate Artemis has in store for me becomes clear. The task she sets me is to be mentor and guide to the Captain and Zanthoula as they sail the seven seas on the good ship *Cappelle*. My destiny is to be a Ship's Cat. (I am also, it seems, to become a diarist!)

And so my diary begins: I draw the line at the "Day One, Day Two" approach, for days can be boringly routine – but intend to make a sequential record of matters of interest, to include my thoughts, memories and personal opinions.

New Year's Day is significant, not just for the commencement of my diary, but for me nearly losing the tip of my tail. Admittedly feeling rather full of myself, I opt to trespass on the boat next door (a fishing tramp piled with any old iron) on a sortie of discovery to poke about a bit while the German tinkers, who man it, are ashore. Presuming the craft unoccupied, I am in for a shock, for Alsatian Guard Dog, Wolfgang, remains at home. (I should have remembered that it is curiosity that killed the cat.) Wolfgang is as surprised to see me as I am to see him. I have never scarpered so fast in my life and feel lucky to have retained the tip of my tail. (Actually Wolfgang turns out to be an old softie and very lonely. He is never taken for walks and takes to trailing Zanthoula, if given half a chance, when she goes out shopping.)

It is not long before the scent of spring is in the air. The sap rising, I become aware of a tingle in the blood. This is probably what leads me to venture onto *terra firma* for the very first time of my own accord, for no particular reason, except that I catch a glimpse of a ditzy little dolly-cat who, methinks, raises her tail!) It only takes a moment to cross to the rocks and race up the sea wall to the feral cat caves, which house the lucky survivors of the council slaughter. This results in a regular routine of me scampering off after breakfast to pay the Mandraki Harlequins a social call – we dub them the Harlequins because of their coats of many colours.)

I am always back for tea, except once when, in my absence, our line-up is placed under Harbour Master's orders to move down quay to make room for a holiday flotilla. (Flotillas take precedence over private craft.) When I return from my dalliance ashore it is to find *Cappelle* vanished into thin air. Imagine the horror! Where my sovereign territory should have been, empty water gleams. The situation is saved by Denise, mother of the missing Zéus, who spots me staring aghast at the apparent watery grave of all I hold most dear. Off she goes to report the situation to my

Pets. "Your leetle cat, 'e look the water!" she tells them. The Captain sets out hot foot to fetch me. Sensibly, he refrains from picking me up, but makes me follow in his footsteps to *Cappelle*'s new berth on strict instructions to remember every inch of the way. Discipline on *Cappelle* is Draconian. The Captain runs a tight ship. If he catches me snagging the furled genoa with my claws, I get my ears boxed. (And so it should be; indiscipline on a ship is not to be tolerated.)

Anyway, I am happy to record, the flotilla incident is the last time I get lost. From then on my sense of self-preservation burgeons. "Η ζωή καλή είναι!" ("Life is good!) Many years of enjoyment are anticipated. No point in cutting my time short. I only behave injudiciously once when, returning from the cat caves, I am panicked by a dog. This leads to misjudgement of the jump home. Fortunately, I manage to save myself a ducking by clinging to the fender of the boat next door. This incident persuades my Pets to purchase a stout fishing net on a long cane in case I should ever fall in. I don't. (Well, not for a long time anyway.)

My rising sap has a consequence. I am to undergo an important rite of passage. "All part of growing up!" they say. (Not much sympathy there then.) It seems, as Ship's Cat, I am not to be given the chance of establishing a Wacky dynasty. Life is to become serious. An appointment is made in town with Adrianos the Vet. My Pets pack me into a holdall with my head sticking out and we are on our way. (Not exactly a dignified mode of travel, but at least I can see where I am going.)

Somewhere in the Old City, we enter a room called a Waiting Room. Here an old lady chats about her cats, who are 'on the pill'. (The Greek for "pill" is "το χάπι", pronounced "happy" in English. Human beans find this a huge joke.) The scene in the room known as the surgery beyond is eye-popping. "As busy as Clapham Junction," the Captain calls it. All the world is there, milling about socialising. Animal cut-outs and icons decorate the walls, while Teddy bears from the vet's nursery days are placed at "cuddle-me" pick-up points. A battered refrigerator stands in a corner, together with a desk that has seen better days. An operating table spread with old newspapers, plus two armchairs with the stuffing spilling out, complete the picture. Zanthoula describes the atmosphere as that of a jolly Junior Common Room. A builder's mate, who has suffered an argument with an adze, he tells us, strides in, his hand dripping blood. The three cartons of cigarettes tucked under his arm are in payment for medical treatment. "Always I come to Adrianos! Hospitals is for aspirin!" he whispers to the Captain. His carer is his sheepdog, Rastus.

There is plenty to take my mind off my pre-med. Seeing me about to have my operation, Rastus, ears pricked, rests his chin on the operating table. Everyone gathers round. Total exposure! Most embarrassing! The whole situation is appalling! I just have time to hear Adrianos, about to administer anaesthetic, say, "Not too much! Same as baby! Otherwise might die!" when I am not there anymore. (These are NOT comforting last words to hear just as one falls unconscious.) Afterwards I am told how much everyone enjoyed my op. Needless to say, I did not!

After making a precise incision in one of my scrotal sacs (Ugh!) Adrianos, I was told, declaring, "One penis!" tweezered out a tiny testicle displaying it with a flourish to the assembled throng before dropping it into a chipped enamel bowl. Then, announcing, "Two penis!" he incised the second sac (Ugh! Ugh!) before extracting its goody, which he again brandished in front of the fascinated gathering before stitching my wound with gut. This is also a source of great entertainment to the human beans.

As soon as my heartbeats become regular, my Pets are told it is OK to lay me in my holdall. I am to remain in a darkened room (i.e. cabin), there are to be no loud noises (which might cause a shock to the system) and I am to be given nothing by mouth. Later, sweetened tea with milk, is to be administered to me as a stimulant (delicious, most refreshing), and my wound sprayed with antiseptic powder.

Gaby, concerned for my welfare, brings yeast treats, which he calls *antibiotiques*. Spatially disorientated on regaining consciousness, I have to be restrained from leaping imaginary gaps.

That evening we are invited to dine on *Buckingham Palace*. My Pets are reluctant to accept this invitation so soon after my ordeal, but Sam's people are adamant, since they wish to play me a Billabong song

After my heartbeats slow down I make a good recovery from my operation.

about Bill the Cat. With a chorus of "MEEOOWW! MEEOOWW!" this unpleasant ditty tells of the unfortunate Bill's appointment at the surgery, and centres on his Pet,

"Who, to Bill's regret, left Bill's balls with the family vet!"

I feel the whole episode uncalled for. We leave early.

By the following day I have recovered enough to give my Pets the slip and escape to the rocks where I bump about on my bottom trying to rid myself of the stitchery. This behaviour causes a couple from a Dormobile to follow me about trying to find out what ails me. Twelve days later Adrianos snips out my drawn-thread work and I am myself again, older, wiser, more mature and raring to get to grips with life.

FOUR

Graduation

In which I am granted a WHO Passport.
I graduate as Ship's Cat.
We sail for Cyprus.

Since I am to take up a career as Ship's Cat, the Captain insists I acquire a Certificate of Competence. Not a mere "Competent Crew" qualification, you understand, but a sort of RYA Yachtmaster (Offshore) Feline Proficiency Test. I am quick, I am keen, I am willing to learn. Moreover I am as ticketty-boo as taramasalata. Where diligence is called for, I am your cat. Of course, it is no problem for me to race up the mast. (I could even come down backwards at a pinch.) Though fashioned in boxed spruce, rather than the Kefalonian pine used by Odysseus, ours is still forty feet of traditional wooden mast my claws can latch onto. I could be up there in a jiffy.

In addition to general knowledge I must become acquainted with skippering, close quarters handling under sail, plus navigation and pilotage by day and night. I should also acquire a thorough understanding of longitude and latitude, plus proficiency in man and cat overboard recovery, and overall yacht management.

It is my intention to begin my professional life by playing to my own particular skills – watch-keeping, astro-navigation and, of course, defence of sovereign territory, with particular attention to the welfare of the crew.

I am pretty sure I shall soon master nautical flag codes, since I can already distinguish a number of yachts by their national flags. I can recognise a red ensign as also the blue and white stripes of the Greek flag. Although the Stars & Stripes of the USA are distinctive, some flags are more taxing. The German and Belgian flags, for instance, are easily confused, the German black, red and yellow in horizontal stripes, the Belgian black, yellow and red in vertical stripes. (Skippers could be touchy if you muddle the national identity of their flags.)

One of the first tasks I set myself is to become familiar with the international nautical code alphabet. This is primarily in order to work out how to spell my name in case I am ever called upon to lend assistance to another ship.

Next Zanthoula orders me personal address stickers and enlists me in the Royal Navy (lower ranks – accelerated advancement considered).

Finally, a further appointment is made with Adrianos for the rabies

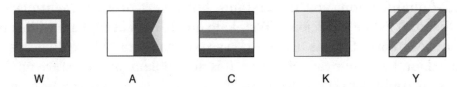

W   A   C   K   Y

and feline leukaemia injections that entitle me to the World Health Organisation Passport, the International Certificate of Vaccination for Cats. Following the code of the Office of Epizootics, this allows me to travel from country to country, so long as I pass their border checks.

Our quay now rings with hammering, shouting, banter and, above all, the noise of boat engines under test. If there is one thing I can't stand it is the roar of a yacht engine! Ours shakes *Cappelle* from stem to stern, makes our bones rattle and gives me the collywobbles. The sight of the Captain about to switch the engine on sets my teeth on edge and sends me squeezing behind the spare water tank to crouch with my paws over my ears.

INTERNATIONAL CERTIFICATE OF VACCINATION

CERTIFICAT INTERNATIONAL DE VACCINATION

INTERNATIONALER IMPFPASS

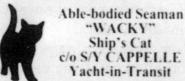

**Able-bodied Seaman
"WACKY"
Ship's Cat
c/o S/Y CAPPELLE
Yacht-in-Transit**

for CATS   **für KATZEN**

This certificate follows the code of the **INTERNATIONAL OFFICE OF EPIZOOTICS,** based on principles laid down by Expert Committees of the **WORLD HEALTH ORGANIZATION** and the **FOOD AND AGRICULTURE ORGANIZATION OF THE UNITED NATIONS**

Ce certificat est conforme aux prescriptions de l'**OFFICE INTERNATIONAL DES ÉPIZOO-TIES,** basées sur les principes formulés par des comités d'experts de l'**ORGANISATION MONDIALE DE LA SANTÉ** et de l'**ORGANISATION DES NATIONS UNIES POUR L'ALIMENTATION ET L'AGRICULTURE**

Dieser Paß entspricht den Vorschriften des **INTERNATIONALEN TIERSEUCHENAMTES** und den von Expertenkomitees der **WELTGESUNDHEITSORGANISATION** und der **WELT-ERNÄHRUNGS- UND LANDWIRTSCHAFTSORGANISATION DER VEREINTEN NATIONEN** festgelegten Richtlinien

A 30912

Hi Ho! Departure looms. Hold onto your hats! We are about to set sail. Gaby's English is now almost as good as mine. In recognition of this the Gauthier family presents us with generous parting gifts, a drum of Turkish honey, twenty litres of wine and six bottles of French champagne (bottled in Rhodes). Gaby's personal gift to me is a jar of tadpoles. I assure him I will send him a postcard decorated with one of my special stickers and promise to see him again soon. I also have farewells to make to Ὁ Γλάρος Ἰάωναδαν (whose other name is "Jonathan Livingston Seagull") with whom I developed a friendship. He promises to follow us out to sea and give *Cappelle* a parting wing waggle, but says he won't come further because, what with all the tourists, the pickings on Rhodes are too good to sacrifice.

I have kept up my watch-keeping practice from my favourite vantage point, the boom, and now know where everything is stored – including my cat biscuits. (Everything in its place and a place for everything.) I have also geared myself, in theory anyway, once out at sea, to pay round-the-clock attention to matters nautical.

Embarking on my very first sea voyage, I pay due heed when the Captain raises the mainsail in gathering darkness as we nose out on a course of 110 degrees for Cyprus. All our friends come to see us off, jumping up and down and waving their arms, even the woman with the coterie of Spanish rescue dogs, who bark and wag their tails. Then, high in the evening air comes the cry I am waiting for: "Καλή νύχτα! Καλό ταξίδι!" ("Good night! Good journey!") It is Jonathan Livingston Seagull's goodbye! We are on our way! Filling in my diary must wait.

I already know that the azure main is cold, wet and wobbly, with a bitter, saline taste, but the comforting way it cradled *Cappelle* in its arms in harbour made up for everything. Here, entirely surrounded by water and out of sight of land, I can see how impossibly big the sea is. Water without bounds! I could never have imagined it could be so vast. When you are flying through the skies on a broomstick you see the land and islands spread out below like a magic map. But at sea level the reality is different. I must confess to letting out a prolonged howl, *"MEOOW –*

OW – OW –!" to warn my Pets about the predicament in which we find ourselves. Somehow, I also believe, that if only I can make Artemis hear, she will take pity and swoop to my rescue. But nothing happens, except that Zanthoula gathers me up and stuffs me inside her Puffa jacket, where I fall asleep.

In the glorious sunrise a school of sea creatures rises from the deep, gambolling and showing off, giving big happy grins before diving only to break surface again to tease us, urging us to play too. "Ooh look! Dolphins!" cries Zanthoula joyfully. If these graceful creatures so enjoy life, that of a sailor can't be so bad, I think, daring to crawl out of Zanthoula's Puffa for a look round. The sea is blue and perfectly flat, the breeze light, the sun sparkling. Our sails flutters like butterfly wings. Are we making progress? It is hard to tell, because, if we are, we carry the full circle of the horizon with us. *Cappelle* is the centre of an annular plate. It is a place of uncertainty nonetheless, dependent on leeway, drift, and our own attention to chart reading. I must remember all I have learned.

Pointing to the east, my Pets meet in urgent discussion. Following Zanthoula's finger, I see a faint smudge on the port horizon. My heart leaps! It must be a coastline! We are not going to be at sea for ever! We alter course for a closer look. According to our plotted course we are now south of the notorious Seven Capes on the Turkish mainland. But Zanthoula, from memory of a previous passage, believes the capes lie yet ahead.

We sail on.

FIVE

Danger

In which we make landing on Kastellorizzo.
I fear drowning when a squall strikes.

The spring sun burns. On a perfect midday we tie up opposite the Restaurant Thalassina in the small harbour of Kastellorizzo, which I am pleased to think of as Swordfish Island since its surrounding waters teem with swordfish. It is the most far-flung of all the Greek islands.

If I despaired of ever touching land again, I need not have worried. Paws on the cap rail, quivering with excitement, I assess my situation, needing to make sure the natives are friendly before disembarking. Even then it takes me half an hour to gather the courage to hop off into the unknown for a quick survey before returning to *Cappelle*, where garrulous swallows, pegged out on the shrouds, are already warning one another the latest arrival in harbour has a cat aboard.

The Port Captain greets the Captain with the words "Welcome, Sir! Here you are Nowhere!" How strange! From Greece to Turkey to Nowhere, all in twenty-four hours! "Nowhere!" because, so far away and close to Turkey, Kastellorizzo remains off most Greek maps. But still a little old lady toils every day to the "Red Castle" to haul up the Greek flag.

That night, satisfied I have memorised my boat's position, and that my Pets have not transported me to a distant island just to dump me –

not that mine would, but I have heard tell of it being the fate of some ill-starred kittens – I leave my ship to socialize. The cats of Kastellorizzo prove a friendly bunch, not averse to a stranger in their midst. "Γειά σου! Hi there, Matey!" they meow cheerfully, "Give us a sea shanty, then!" before being generous enough to show me the rear entrance to the Thalassina from which tender morsels of swordfish and left-over kalamari (a bit chewy but palatable) are thrown. Inside the restaurant in the angles of the ceiling swallows have built their nests. One pair is nesting directly above the juke box. The birds take turns at hatching duties, one partner sitting on the eggs while the other rests on a Campari bottle behind the bar.

Lawrence Durrell described Kastellorizzo as perfect for honeymoons or writing a book. Since sailors have a girl in every port, it is to be no honeymoon for me, but it is a good place for catching up on a diary.

Swordfish Island is a stop-over on our voyage to Cyprus. The Captain is concerned with our lack of speed, since we have averaged only 3.7 knots on the way from Rhodes. Thinking this could be because the hull and propeller are dirty, he dives into harbour to clean them off while I march up and down the side-deck miaowing, "Have you taken leave of your senses?" at the top of my voice. When he clambers aboard, livid with cold, Zanthoula rubs him down and I knead his chest to get his circulation going, before curling up in the crook of his arm to keep him warm.

Immediately after our night sail I note in my diary that true relaxation is part and parcel of the life afloat. But the situation is about to undergo a dramatic change. I hadn't bargained for what happens next.

As we make preparations to leave, Sokrati runs out to say that "bad winds" are forecast. We must delay our departure, he says "if we don't want to lose our sails". (What can he possibly mean?) He will bring us coffee and will cook wild vetch omelettes. We are unsure about his weather warning. All is so far serene. Moreover, we know the islanders welcome *Cappelle* as the only yacht in port and would like us to stay. In any case it cannot be for long, for we have failed to fill our water tank before leaving Rhodes and Kastellorizzo is a waterless island. And we have a rendezvous to keep in Cyprus. On the other hand who could regret another day on Swordfish Island? Certainly not Zanthoula, who, glad of an excuse to remain, is swooning over bougainvillaea-covered pergolas, pools of blue irises, black dragon lilies and such like. Off she goes to climb the heights as far as the prohibited military zone near the summit from which we Greeks keep a wary eye on Turkey. She comes down reporting black clouds gathering over the Turkish mountains. At teatime a sudden hailstorm heaps sizeable pellets of ice in the cockpit. But the storm is short-lived. I have been relying on the antennae at the end of my whiskers and the sensations in my bones for assessment of weather conditions. Now I resolve to undertake a serious study of cloud formation to add meteorology to my skill set.

After a quiet night, the following morning dawns calm and clear. So much for the weather warning! To the south the Aegean stretches placid as a dream on and on to distant Cyprus. A fishing fleet from Kalymnos, a mid-Aegean island, comes in. We can see the crew has taken on a full load of fish and are ready to be on their way but, surprisingly, they stay put. The Captain asks a fisher lad, who consults his uncle. His answer is the Delphic one: if we wish to lose our sails, we should leave! It seems that the fishing fleet's powerful radio transmitters (purchased with EU grants) are picking up the Italian weather bulletin. Swordfish island lies directly in the path of an Atlantic depression that, after deepening in the storm kitchen of the Gulf of Genoa, is tracking our way fast.

"Πάθημα, Μάθημα!" ("One lives and learns!") As well as being on a steep learning curve, we are soon on the crest of a wave as well! When the harbour waters go into convulsions, the fishing fleet quickly moves to anchor off, while we take the ill-considered option of pulling *Cappelle* off the quay on long lines. The sea is choppy, but not too uncomfortable. However, by morning we know we were not leaving any time soon. The Captain has developed a fever and it is already blowing a fresh gale in sea areas Taurus, Delta and Crusade in the path ahead. Now up to speed in the Beaufort Scale (an empirical measurement reckoned by observation), I recognise Gale Force 8.

The in-harbour conditions are soon far from ideal either, since the harbour bears the brunt of down-draughts from the hillside against the west-flowing current. Telling myself not to panic, I am aware of the sudden influx of confused seas from the Turkish Channel and resolve to keep an eye on the warps. All of a sudden *"Sauve qui peut!"* becomes an attractive idea. Grabbing my diary for safe-keeping, I flee through the cabin into the forepeak to squeeze behind the spare water tank. As *Cappelle* buck-jumps on her long lines, Zanthoula gets the engine started. Although she is desperate to release the warps and raise anchor to move off quay, she is task-saturated by having to jam the gear lever into reverse with her knee to prevent it springing out.

This is all too technical for me and I substitute action for a fervent petition to Artemis to do something – and be quick about it. (Needless to say, she does nothing. Is she deaf or something? Can't she SEE we are in trouble? Gossiping with the other goddesses, I'll be bound!) The next thing I know the sea has gone into a paroxysm, a starboard warp snaps and *Cappelle* slews to port. Yelling *"Οχτό Μποφόρ στο λιμάνι!"* ("Full gale in harbour!") the fishermen line up to try to prevent us hitting the quay beam on. At this point the Captain staggers ghost-like out of his bed of sickness as a wall of spume roars in and crashes down on top of us, enveloping our world and smothering us under mountainous seas.

The quay's low elevation is our salvation, for the giant wave does not pause to break and backlash, but sweeps on unimpeded, allowing *Cappelle* to resurface, bows digging – it is me inside there down under somewhere, don't forget! – to pitch like a bronco on a six to eight feet swing. (A bumpy ride! That's what life's about!) At this climatic moment, catching the momentum in a godlike effort as the stern rises again, the white-faced Captain materialises. He heaves in the anchor, riding weight and all, just as the remaining long-line snaps. Then he slams the ship into reverse, yanking her off the quay, engages forward gear and, in one sweeping movement, wrenches the bows hard over to port to roar into a turn in which we miss the stone pier by a hair's breadth.

Whew! This is my baptism as Ship's Cat. Swilling about in the briny that fills the forepeak after my Big Dipper ride, I do not even know which way is up! How anxious my Pets must be about me, I think, wetly and woozily, as I crawl out. But so occupied have they been with more pressing matters, they have not even spared me a thought. Look after Number One! That's the ticket. No one else will! "Good to see you, Wacky!" says Zanthoula after a while, a tad too casually, methinkst.

As, after anchoring off, *Cappelle* rocks violently in the subsiding waves, boats are forgotten, for the Restaurant Thalassina – or rather the pile of wreckage where her dining room once stood – takes precedence. Thalassina has taken the full brunt of the sea. Brick walling is reduced to rubble. Heavy duty metal columns lie mangled and all-weather roofing flaps crazily, torn to shreds. On the quay, breakers, losing their power, corkscrew through broken brickwork, smashed floodlights, jagged lumps of concrete and tangled wiring. What has Sokrati, Thalassina's owner, done to deserve this? He is not insured. But, he shrugs philosophically. "Ετσι η ζωή – Such is life!" We are all in the lap of the gods! That goes for me too, I think bitterly. The fishermen muscle in to manhandle Sokrati's pile of debris to a back street before drying out their boats, as we do *Cappelle*. Tomorrow is another day.

The following afternoon, in conditions as serene as those that preceded the squall, Cappelle troops out, bringing up the rear behind the fishing fleet.

SIX

A Greeting from the Red Arrows

In which the Red Arrows bid us welcome.

I enjoy life at the Sheraton.

I meet an evil tomcat and make canine cronies.

At midnight Zanthoula fastens on her safety harness, then, armed
with a torch and thermos, she takes charge of *Cappelle*. She
always was a fusspot and seems to think I might fall overboard,
so my movements are circumscribed. Confined to a restricted area of
the deck, I set about watch-keeping, knowing that, if I stray, Zanthoula
will nab me by the scruff and chuck me into the cabin.

At all times I must keep a wary eye on shipping. I have learned the
difference between the port light (red) and the starboard light (green)
and have memorised useful couplets concerning collision courses:

"If to starboard red appear, 'tis your duty to keep clear."

"Green to green and red to red, perfect safety, go ahead!"

I must also keep a weather eye on Zanthoula to make her aware should
she miss something significant. Sometimes *Cappelle* gives way to other
shipping. (Sadly, my countrymen are not reliable about obeying the rules.)
Steam should give way to sail, but you never know. Remember Michael

O'Day "who died maintaining the right of way!" Ships' Cats must keep their wits about them!

The sea at night is magic. In my diary I wax poetic. A crescent moon balances by its tip on the surface of the sea before being slowly sucked in. Then the Morning Star blazes out like a white searchlight. At 5 a.m. we hoist the Cypriot flag. But it is long hours under sail before we enter Paphos. There is no time to go ashore and introduce myself to the natives, as I am anxious to do, knowing I might have Cypriot blood – there is a story that at the end of the Aegean War the starving Italian soldiers on Rhodes found themselves obliged to eat cats. Such was the subsequent shortage of cats, that, when the war ended, the islanders imported shiploads of felines from Cyprus to keep down the rat population. Such cats may have been my forebears!

There follows a night sail to the Sheraton marina in Limassol. At 03.30 hrs Cape Aspro gleams white without benefit of moonlight. It is on rounding the cape in the grey light of dawn that the welcome to end all glorious welcomes occurs. I am sitting on the coach roof when the air is compressed with a beehive roar as the Red Arrows trailing red, white and blue streamers take off from their Sovereign Air Base at Akrotiri to execute their classic trademark, the Diamond Nine, right over our heads – just for *Cappelle*, the only ship at sea! What a greeting for a small British yacht! I raise a paw in salute. (I hope they saw me.)

We are nicely berthed at the Sheraton beside the motor cruiser which Aristotle Onassis gave his daughter, Christina, for her seventeenth birthday. We are immediately made welcome by our live-aboard neighbours, who rush up to spill the beans about a certain Lord Byron (a tyrant tomcat). Apparently His Lordship, who is under the delusion of owning the Sheraton, is presently away cruising on his super-yacht *No More Mr Nice Guy*. Defensive action must be taken on his return, my Pets are warned, or he will "have your pretty kitty's guts for garters".

Meanwhile I am in splendid form. According to the marina rulebook, domestic pets "must be kept on board at all times". In practice the marina is a menagerie. I fly up and down its pontoons with wings on my feet.

To starboard lives Bessie, a sweet-natured doormat of a Pyrenean Mountain Dog dumped off a yacht when she grew too big for it. The Pets who took her in did everything they could to make up for her ill-treatment, squeezing up to give her a whole berth to herself. On our other side lives Jo-Jo, a good friend of mine, a lion-hearted little Sealyham from Beirut. We play chase. Most of the animals in the marina began life as outcasts. Being British, most yacht owners soon lose their hearts to some less fortunate fellow creature. Bessie and Jo-Jo are kind enough to take upon themselves the duty of minding me. Both break into frantic barking whenever His Byronic Lordship shows his whiskers, which he frequently does on his return, until Zanthoula gets the measure of him. Even then he stalks up unsheathing his tiger claws and wicked teeth in readiness to snick, snack, snook. It requires several squirts from Zanthoula's pressure hose to settle his hash. The first time he puts in an appearance he has sneaked on deck before Zanthoula even notices. When she grabs the boat hook, he stands his ground, spitting and swearing at her in a most unaristocratic manner. (Humble beginnings there, all right!)

We are a close community at the Sheraton, an international No Man's Land where boats fly no flags. The shooting dead of innocent live-aboards (and their dog) in nearby Larnaca marina is an act of terrorism still vivid in the memory. The guards in desert uniform, who patrol the concourse in our protection, carry Armalite rifles. I mind my ps and qs and they take no notice of me. Not even a pot shot, I am glad to report.

I discover a new game, which is to pop through the porthole bearing small fry to crunch on the carpet. I cheat a bit sometimes, I must admit. I am congratulated on the quality of my catch, but it is not long before my Pets notice some of it presents a slightly sun-baked appearance. My secret is out when it is discovered these fish are hand-line discards. Once I drag home a sizeable sardine given me by a fisherman, laying it beside Zanthoula's berth as a surprise for her when she wakes up. It is a surprise all right! Unfortunately, she swings her legs out with her eyes shut and steps on my offering barefoot. Oh dear!

My Pets buy me goodies from a proper pet shop that opens in Limassol, the first such outlet in the islands, with a whole section devoted to cats. As well as worm pills (Yuck!) on which Zanthoula insists, they acquire, best of all, trays of an exquisite gourmet cat food called "Pourquoi je t'aime", a heaven-sent delicacy that truly makes my whiskers curl. "*Bon appétit!*" they say as they dish it out. When I note this French phrase in my diary (you never know in which country a Ship' Cat might end up) I am glad to see my paw-writing coming along splendidly.

So far, everywhere we go, I could happily settle. But boat people are peripatetic by nature. Even if you do not vacate a berth yourself, your friends move on. Early one morning, after an evening spent by the Captain concentrating on the relevant weather forecasts and on serious chart consultation, we leave Cyprus. Bessie has already gone. Jo Jo, while wishing me well, tells me the signs are that he is about to leave too. We all pray that Lord Byron will get his comeuppance and drown horribly in a vat of ouzo.

SEVEN

Heavy Weather

In which we endure heavy weather in the Gulf of Antalya.
We revisit Kastellorizzo.

The Captain is up at four in the morning to collect the passports and check out of the Sheraton, so that we can be well offshore before contrary winds get up. We sail away on a greasy sea under a greasy sky. Dolphins do their thing. A cloud of flying fish glides by and we pass the floating body of a dead hawk. At Aphrodite's Rocks, their feet swirling with sea wrack, we bid farewell to Cyprus. Fifteen miles out, a small bird perches on the jib sheet. Knowing I can't reach it, it laughs at me.

Our trip is pretty routine so far. That evening the sun sinks in a salmon-pink sky. It is sometime after midnight before the wind freshens, more energy entering the system. Seeing us seriously over-canvassed, I give the Captain a nip on the ankle. He at once yells for his sea boots and for assistance in reefing. Zanthoula, half-asleep, muttering crossly, "I'll give you boots!" yanks the offending footwear out of the wet wardrobe, spilling paraffin in her haste to throw them on deck. She'd better calm down, I think to myself. We all need to pull our weight.

Oh dear! Sailors should, of course, as I had been trying to point out, anticipate the need to reef well before the task becomes imperative. It is tempting, but foolhardy, to delay for the simple reason you are on course and sailing boldly; a situation can rapidly deteriorate. Zanthoula, battling to hold the mainsail into wind, hung onto the down hauls, while the beleaguered Captain made Herculean efforts lying on his back on the coach roof, to tie reefing strings in pitching darkness. It took him long blankety-blank minutes to fix a double slab reef in the main. Then, more easily, he reduces the genoa to a fraction of its normal size.

Slithering about in the rising wind, buffeted this way and that, slipping and sliding, hanging on by my toe nails, I confess to being tempted to add my chorus to the mad night as we pound through a wet lunar landscape gouged and deformed by a gusting north westerly. Then Zanthoula nabs me by the scruff and shoves me rudely into the forepeak, slamming the doors. Of course, the rhythmless slap of the bows soon burst them open again and I escape, curiosity overcoming anxiety.

A confused pattern of white-capped peaks erupting in pyramids as they surge towards the Gulf of Antalya (known as a Mediterranean Bay of Biscay) confronts me. A bristling mass of water mountains, deep, obstacle-strewn gullies, foaming chasms, rearing sea towers, black holes and pinched water canyons hold us in thrall. A series of crazily solid, ever-changing shapes form a watery alpine wilderness. Moonlit overhangs of giant waves, acting in synergy with their wind shadows to steal the power from our sails are hell-bent on forcing us out of control. An incantation of mine is "algorithmic ineptitude". I haven't the slightest idea what it means, but it rolls nicely off the tongue and I repeat it as a mantra in times of stress.

After this it is hard going to pick up our course again. When we do so, we are constantly forced off it, plunging and jouncing, taking water across the deck and ploughing through sea cavities. That is the first night. Daylight brings a small windshift in our favour. When Zanthoula knocks off on the afternoon of the second day, she takes me with her, clutched to her chest. We lie on her berth hugging each other, ever aware of chaotic seas pounding along the side deck close to our ears. Night descends. Another dawn follows. Time becomes meaningless. Sometimes we snatch food or drink. "Must keep rehydrated!" orders the Captain sensibly. When Zanthoula takes the next watch I go with her.

With conditions marginally improved, I have a quiet word with my muse, Urania, to seek her advice on astronavigation. All she does is whisper in my ear to get a grip. I see we have torn a reefing point. Then the Captain details us to look out for a rogue oil drum he thinks he spotted. It could damage our propeller and should be fended off, he shouts. What a laugh! Neither of us ever see it. Zanthoula staggers about making coffee while I lap water and crunch cat biscuits. Who'd be a sailor! But when you're in the thick of it, you're right in it, and there is nothing to be done but to grit your teeth and do your best to stay on top of the situation.

By the following morning we are out of the worst of the turbulence and on auto-helm. Life begins to look reasonable again. Filling in my diary soothes me. The sea has calmed to a flaccid swell, the sky has cleared to a myopic aquamarine and the immediate past is fading into an exhausting blur. I perch in the bows, my eyes fixed on the forward horizon. No land in sight. Then I choke on something I am trying to say, which comes out as a squawk. "Ship's Cat wants to tell us something," calls the Captain. "Go and see what's he's on about." The words that stuck in my throat were, "LAND AHOY!" I thought I had caught sight of something on the forward horizon more solid than a band of mist.

From the shore the sea is fluid, while, from the tossing waters of confused seas, advancing and receding, shifting and changing, portions sliding in and out like shutters as mutable as a stage set on rollers, it is the land that is liquid. Nothing exists of itself. Mountains wander about while deceiving islands appear and disappear. Zanthoula identifies a low-lying cigar shape that has to be Kekova. To its west must lie the island of Kastellorizzo for which we are bound. But from our angle Swordfish Island now blends in with the island of Strongli in an altogether different identity.

Having better recollection of the navigable passages into Kastellorizzo's archipelago, to which most entrances are false and whose mini-headlands conceal underwater reefs, Zanthoula takes over inshore navigation. So we wind our way through skerries that shimmer with a million shattered mirrors floating in the lime-lit shallows of speedwell blue water, me, with the Captain's help, miaowing "PORT", "STARBOARD", "SLOW DOWN" or "PORT HAND DOWN A BIT", as the case might be.

As Zanthoula brings us safely into harbour, *Cappelle* is recognised. A reception committee gathers. Sokrati runs forward to help. A visiting yachtswoman takes Zanthoula's hand to assist her ashore. "You look TERRIBLE, dear!" she says. What about me? Nobody pays attention to a Ship's Cat. But then Sokrati brings a tasty morsel and I know what a joy it is to be back on Swordfish Island.

Before I hop ashore to look up old acquaintances and regale them with further mariner's tales, the Captain, who has wolfed down a whole packet of Cypriot chocolate biscuits, tells the skipper of *Ciccellino*, to the latter's surprise, we have taken thirty hours (a day, a night and half a day) to sail to Kastellorizo from Limassol. This goes to show how the passing of time can deceive, even (oddly enough) shorten, under stress. In fact our passage, as I well know, has taken fifty-five hours and fifteen minutes, or two days, two nights and half a day, a more realistic span in which to sail 220 nautical miles by small boat. The worst of the conflicting seas lasted thirteen hours.

My friends and I schedule our sea shanties and Greek dancing for when the moon rises. First the cabin must be set to rights and aired. At present it reeks of the paraffin Zanthoula spilt when she dragged out the Captain's sea boots, plus suppurating rabbit stew, prepared but never consumed. It is so far gone that even I don't fancy it. ("Ça pue," – "It stinks") I say, practising my French, a paw to my nose.

EIGHT

A Hilarious Dinner Party

In which Gaby and family entertain us to dinner.
We leave for the Dodecanese Islands

Two days later we leave Kastellorizzo en route, via Rhodes, to see Gaby, for the Dodecanese island of Samos to meet family and friends. Though other yachts turn into Yali Liman on the coast of Turkey (illegal without official entry to Turkey but usually accepted) to await the optimum hour of four in the morning to tackle passage of the Seven Capes, we head straight out to sea.

Off the Çatal Islands, beating into Force 6, the "yachtsman's gale", we hold our own, while to starboard battalions of white horses gallop in dazzling sunshine towards the Sands of Patara. I am already wearing my safety harness when Zanthoula shouts to the Captain to buckle up, a moment before, drenched by an overspill, he misses his footing.

The only way to force forward progress is to claw off the Sands of Patara in a series of tacks, the next tack bringing us back almost onto our original position. This area is where the beautiful witch Olympias once rose from the sea disguised as a mermaid to demand news of her son, Alexander the Great. "Come on! Let's shout!" the Captain mouths and we shout above the tumult the answer that saved the fisherman from drowning: "Ο Μεγαλέχανδρος...ζεῖ...και βασιλεύει!" – "Alexander the Great...lives...and reigns!" The stirring syllables, echoing to the Seven

Capes, bounce back. This is a sign our exhortation is heeded. On the stern, its bungees stretched to breaking point, the bin for the anchor chain jumps wildly, before, with a snap of its restraining cords, it spills its contents. Somehow we drag the chain out of the sea, while cheering the empty bin as it takes to the air, somersaulting into the sky. If this is the spell that calmed the raging waters for the fisherman, it also worked for us.

Even though I had played my part in influencing the waves, my Pets confine me to the forepeak "for my safety" (as per usual), while they heave to, to adjust sail and change tack. (Sailing lee rail under never makes for faster progress.) But confinement is naught for my comfort. The cabin is a tip. Seawater, siphoning through the sink outlet, floods the galley and I haven't fared much better in the forepeak, as my Pets discovered when they let me out after we forged parallel with the Bad Cape, last of the Seven, in a final surfing zigzag. My coat is spiked with sea water and I am soaked to the skin. All their fault, of course! This is gospel truth, since they forgot to put a bung in the navel pipe to the chain locker! The look in my eyes tells them what I think of the oversight.

There are times when I would give anything not to have signed on for a sailor! After all, there are more enviable careers for a Likely Lad, apprenticeship to a fishmonger, for example, or the post of Chief Mouser in a bake house. Anything but forcible incarceration in a fore-cabin under a cold shower. At least Zanthoula gives me a rubdown with my special towel. (Being a cat I lack the capacity to giggle. I envy whose who can when rub-a-dubbed with a towel. It does tickle so!)

We cannot take out the final reef because the roll of sail covers the tear in the sail we acquired, but the Captain succeeds in setting us on course for Rhodes. Then Zanthoula and I take the midnight watch. It is the clearest of nights and she steers by an arbitrary star, me tucked inside her Puffa. We know we mustn't nod off, but stay on red alert for:

"The seas are lonely, dark and deep
But we have promises to keep
And miles to go before we sleep..."

At dawn Rhodes appears on the horizon. I was looking forward to seeing Gaby again, but the faces in Mandraki are those of strangers. The new crowd has moved in. Zanthoula rushes me to Adrianos, who is engaged in stitching a puppy's ear, for my feline influenza booster. All haste then ceases as Adrianos and Zanthoula sit down to nibble pumpkin seeds and chat.

The Captain returns waving a bouquet of "Welcome back!" roses from Gaby and the news that Daniel, has agreed to urgent sail repair by courtesy of the Gauthier's newly opened *Voilerie Gauthier* (Sail Repair Loft). Moreover, the Captain has also arranged for Camper & Nicholson to fly *Cappelle* in a new hyper-quality flexible steel exhaust section from Athens on the morrow, and we are to dine with the Gauthiers that night.

We take a taxi to the Old City, since Zanthoula, suffering from sea legs, twists her ankle in the engine cavity. It can't take us all the way to the Gauthier apartment, which is situated in a maze of intersecting donkey paths, but the driver sets us down beside a big iron gate where Gaby awaits us on his bicycle.

Drinks are served in the Gauthier's moonlit garden-cum-*potager* beside a blazing log fire heaped in an old iron bath. Bonne Mère, Mireille's straight-backed Mama from Marseilles, joins the party. Wrapped in shawls, she says how much she enjoys the Greek islands but that evening chill in the islands makes her teeth chatter. (I recommend a fur coat.)

We barbecue lamb kebabs with garlic sauce. As I am becoming quite a foodie I am given a whole kebab to myself to gnaw under the medlar tree beside the goldfish pond. "Don't touch the goldfish, Wacky!" (As if I would, I know my manners!) It is a hilarious reunion. All the human beans act pretty silly in a happy sort of way, knocking back French champagne and sipping cognac out of cracked egg-cups. I stay sober, of course. (Somebody has to.) The dining room, where we take our first and second rounds of kebab, is a conversion from a mediaeval cistern. Entry is down steps, not to a water storage pool, but to a table set with flowers in a broken jug around which the human beans perch on wobbly deck chairs tied together with string. Meanwhile Belle Mère, ever obsessed with the niceties, causes hilarity by making a fuss about her inability to provide matching dinner napkins. Pudding is mandarin oranges marinated in rum topped with a dollop of thick cream. I am given a cream mountain to myself.

By the time the Gauthiers have related the story of how they acquired their furniture from rubbish dumps, and described how the lavatory cistern emptied itself on Daniel's head when the chain was pulled, and how the armoire – found to be pinned to the wall with two picture hooks – collapsed on top of Mireille when she opened its door, everybody was crying with laughter. It's a wonder I was able to steer my Pets home. I was sure Baby Simon must have missed his sky-cot suspended from *Baraka's* ceiling. But now he had a bedroom of his own and a Greek girl to nanny him. Mireille's treadle machine, used for sail repair, was sited in an adjacent barn now adopted by the Gauthiers as a sail loft. The flotilla has already taken out a sail-repair contract and the Gauthiers' future looks bright. Baraka was to remain in harbour as a second home until such time as she was needed.

Daniel makes an excellent job of repairing our sail. Then, with the forecast of a smooth barometric field, we are off on another night sail to keep our rendezvous in Samos. Night sailing is, of course, my forte, thanks to my broomstick training and the fact that my nocturnal vision requires only one sixth of the light level demanded by human beans (not everybody knows this).

After negotiating two cruise liners, four tankers and a car ferry, the dying sun finds us abeam Cape Krio as darkness closes in. Here my Pets pour a sundowner and raise a libation to Aphrodite Euploia of Knidos, Aphrodite of Fair Sailing, for safe passage through the night. Before we have reached the far side of the Gulf of Gökova night has fallen. It is one thing to study coded light systems on a chart and quite another to distinguish them in practice. Noting to port the profounder darkness of the bulk of the island of Pserimos, my Pets are unaware of its close proximity until alerted by my wail of caution. When my experienced eyes pick up lamp-black patches to starboard, I call out due warning of the Loch Ness Monster humps of unlit islets. Such waters are no place for a small boat on such a Hecate night – unless, of course, it is served by a Ship's Cat such as me!

When Kalimnos looms, its attendant light structure some way off, the Captain, suspecting the presence of a reef, alters course. At around four in the morning, Zanthoula, staring wide-eyed into the darkness on the look-out for Gaidharos light, dozes off. My howl of protest brings the Captain out in alarm to slam the helm hard over. We are heading straight for the shallows! I know at once that it was Aphrodite Euploia who alerted me to danger.

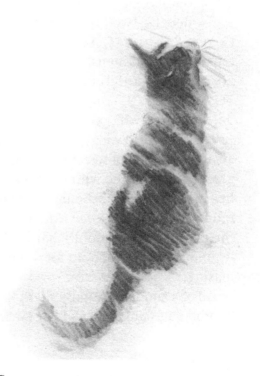

NINE

A Night Sail in Tandem

In which we reunite with old friends.
Golden Prospect joins *Cappelle* on a night sail to Chios.
We gain an escort battleship.

Next day we tie up in Pythagorio, the main harbour of Samos, after our 120-mile passage from Rhodes, discovering in situ, to our delight, two boats out of Rhodes familiar to us – *River Rat* and *Golden Prospect*. The extravagance of our greetings displeases the Port Captain, who admonishes us publicly through his megaphone, "Look after boat first, please! Talk to friends later. AND TELL THAT SHIP'S CAT TO PIPE DOWN." Dogs on leads pass along the quay and a man in a top hat with a tall whip and high-stepping pony drives by in a hackney cab.

In Pythagorio we are at the heart of a sophisticated little resort with an ample supply of restaurants with back premises of feline interest. It is great to be reunited with old friends and to be awaiting family. Vanessa has brought her baby son, Alexander, out from London to be with his father Richard on *River Rat*. The baby and I get on famously, playing the noddy-head game. Richard makes an uncalled for joke about isn't it time I was fattened up for a fender? The cheek of it! (I think he was teasing.)

All of a sudden the early flight from Athens zooms overhead and Mel, Zanthoula's daughter, and her boyfriend, Steve, join *Cappelle*. Then it is hugger mugger fun on board. At night I bring in dead beetles to amuse the crew. After a few days of windsurfing and swimming, we are off again, this time accompanied by *Golden Prospect*, who is joining us on a seventy-mile night sail to the island of Chios.

Halfway up the Straits of Samos, we take a break to anchor under sail in secluded Possidonio. (Anchorages may be picturesque, but are not to my fancy if I cannot get ashore.) After a further night sail we expect to reach the uncharted anchorage of Emborio on Chios.

As we nose out of Possidonio after dark, I am the one to spot the presence of five unlit fishing boats. I prepare myself to nip ankles should I suspect we are about to hit trouble. Once, what Steve believes to be an illuminated coastal village, moves out of position transforming itself into a cruise liner in all its glory, looming ever larger as it steamed towards us. When I feel Zanthoula's colours fading (which means she is getting sleepy) I take up position beside her to anticipate any loss of concentration.

The twinkling triangles of our yachts' navigation lights forging along in parallel are a comforting presence in the darkness before the moon rises to flood the scene with its wet light. Next day the Captain's pencil line on the chart leads us, copybook, John "Longitude" Harrison style, straight to the heart of the tiny land-locked cove of Emborio on Chios. But where is *Golden Prospect,* fallen back after radioing her engine is overheating? We row out to look for her. Evening is falling again before both Captains hoist black balls indicating "yachts at anchor". Early next morning I crouch in our new anchor chain bin, keeping a low profile when transfixed by the sight of a man "tenderizing" an octopus on a rock with a big stick. (I don't want him to see me in case he is minded to do any such dreadful thing to ME.)

The old lady in Emborio's general store tickles me behind the ear and insists on serving my Pets βανίλια spoon sweets (sticky white stuff flavoured with vanilla and Chiot mastic accompanied by sparkling glasses of Chiot water) before we set off around Cape Mastiko. She gives a dry spit to ward away evil spirits.

As a sudden squall races across the Cape, we watch *Golden Prospect* ahead heel on a deceptively flat sea for no discernible reason, as if the victim of a playful tug from the Kraken below. But she rights herself and we sail on to Volissos where we tie up beside a sand-hill, a concrete mixer and a pile of building aggregate. A goat, a sick cat and an emaciated donkey approach. Having given the cat a "*Γειά σου!*" ("Hello!") and a "*Πώς έισαι;*" ("How are you?") to which she weakly replies, "*Έτσι κι έτσι*" ("so-so"), saying "*Περαστικά!*" ("Get well soon!") I add, "*Να τα κατοστήσετε!*" ("May you live to be a hundred!") Greek style. I felt sorry for her being so poorly. It is right to observe the courtesies. Then I run to dance a solo *Ζεϊμπέκικο* (a Greek dance) on top of the sand-hill.

After Julia has done her washing under the quayside tap, she and Zanthoula climb to the village on the acropolis to shop for bread and bantam eggs, all that is available there. In the seventeenth century a Scotsman known as "Cut-lugged Willie" (who made his escape to the Greek Islands after dalliance with a lady whose brothers cut off his ears) had trudged the same route.

At the end of the day I accompany the two Captains when they go to consult the local fishermen about weather prospects. If Chiot fishermen are so skilled in the laws of the sea that Christopher Columbus learned the art of navigation from them, who are we to argue? The fishermen give them assurance that, if we delay setting sail until after midnight, the contrary winds, presently blowing, will have dropped.

Our departure is a shambles with the Captain getting a feather of fishhooks stuck in his hand. Then we fall over each other, knocking the anchor chain overboard and arguing in our struggle to raise sail. It struck me there are far too many human beans aboard that night with too many feet. I have a job to keep them all under control as we roll drunkenly on a waterbed of hard lumps to execute a wide sweep in avoidance of rocks and shoals before bearing north. In the event all five of us remain on watch, a pair of eyes to each corner of the compass, so to speak, me in overall position on the coach roof. When turns are taken throughout the night to hot-bunk, I make sure to bag the snuggest spot.

(This reminds me that a favourite word of mine is "catawampus". Not only does it feature both "cat" and "puss" but it describes how I like my beds, all warm and messy and well wriggled on.)

We make sure of frequent checks on the echo sounder to judge our proximity to the rock-girt coastline. To make things even more interesting, we have now picked up a naval escort, a Greek battleship, which was lying in wait outside Volissos to take up our trail. As a pod of dolphins rise with the sun, it is clear the battleship is not to be shaken off, so we proceed under escort as the pyramid of Plomari's coloured houses on Lesbos rise into view like a pretty pop-up book.

When we dock on Sappho's Isle, the battleship docks alongside. Practising leaping on and off *Cappelle* to get my bearings, I am dismayed to hear myself described as being a "demanding little so-an-so" all night. Gimme a break! Don't human beans understand that someone of know-how, such as me, deserves his creature comforts too?

It turns out the sailors on the battleship want to be friends. They also wish to take me on as their Ship's Cat. But I have no desire to transfer to the Greek navy. We barrack them when they are marshalled in line to dive off the stern. Then Steve falls in head first trying to rescue a tea towel, before being hauled back on board in an act of heroic effort by Mel and Zanthoula, who each grab an ankle. The sailors are beside themselves with mirth at this acrobatic display. We expect a twenty-one-gun salute! Afterwards Gary harpoons an monstrous octopus, and my Pets snorkel in a nearby bay until, that is, they discover undeniable evidence of a yacht using it to empty its holding tank. This makes them shriek and scramble out double-quick. (Now I understand why the Owl and the Pussy Cat's boat was pee green!)

Moving on, after Mel and Steve fly home to work, we bid a fond farewell to our mates, the battleship crew, before anchoring in the deserted cove of Mersinia to the tinkle of goat bells. The nights are so glorious that I sleep curled up beneath the stars in the angle between the mast and boom where the main sail folds thickest. A local fisherman, rowing over to cadge a glass of ouzo, advises us to stay on, saying that on every other island it is "Κλέφτη! Κλέφτη!" (They are all thieves and vagabonds, those other islanders – it was ever the way to describe the neighbours!) Someone has painted a dagger dripping blood beside our friend's cottage, accompanied by blink-makingly rude words sprayed Greek-style on the rocks. I am thankful my Pets are not as familiar with the Greek language as I am, for the fisherman is colourfully described as a sodomite, a pimp and the son of a whore. (I blush to think about the rest of the insults.)

Our anchorage may be picturesque but, on the whole, after twice suffering minor indignities, I do not think much of it. When invited to tea on *Golden Prospect* I miss my footing on her slippery sun awning, slide down it on my backside and only just save myself from falling in. (It is simply impossible to make claws stick in kevlar.) To add to this insult, everybody laughs, which is unfair, and makes me think darkly about jumping ship (as if I ever would). The second near mishap occurred after a trip out in the dinghy. On return from this jaunt the Captain rowed us past our ship, in order (he explained later) to turn round and come in alongside. Anxious to get home to look after my biscuits, which have been calling me for some time, I take a leap for the deck as we pass by, an injudicious act, which also almost ends in inundation. They laugh again! Would you believe it? You would think they would have more tact! (I hope Artemis wasn't looking. I suppose she might have found it amusing too.)

TEN

My New Friend

In which I get stuck in the porthole.

I play Sylvester to Tweetie Pie.

I acquire a new best friend.

On arrival in Mitilini we find the citizens discussing an undersea earthquake which caused the harbour water to suck back more than a metre before surging violently in again. Fortunately, there is no repeat of this incident.

A pleasant little garden with a statue of Sappho flanks the quay. Passers-by applaud as I race home after play to dive through the porthole into the cabin. "Like a rabbit down a burrow," they say. However, one day something bad happens. I suspect – whisper it – I must have put on weight, which causes me to GET STUCK (like Winnie the Pooh when he got wedged in the doorway of Rabbit's house after over-indulging on too much honey for elevenses). I push and puff and pull this way and that, making my middle sore, until at last I burst free through the little round window. After this I vow never to venture through a porthole again, and I never have. (Once avoirdupois sets in, it cannot be denied.)

With winds from the Balkans rendering the month of June bitterly cold, people mutter, "Πολυχάλια!" ("Wretched weather!"). We light the Tilley lamp for warmth and snuggle under the duvets. Then, when things take a turn for the better, sailing yacht *Enchanted April* puts in.

As an elderly lady, wearing a floaty dress (not the type of garment one usually associates with boats) and a wide-awake leghorn hat tied on with chiffon, moves forward to step ashore, the Captain hurries to lend her his assistance. But the lady is already opening a gate on the bows. The gentleman with her then thanks the Captain in olde worlde English, saying that, as offers of help are rare in the islands, the gate has been put in for his wife's convenience. The couple are German and come to Lesbos every year to spend time on their boat.

Usually content with a single by-rights inspection of a neighbour, I develop a particular interest in *Enchanted April* on account of a trilling sound of great purity issuing from her interior. In fact, so intrigued am I, I fail to resist camping out on her coach roof with my nose pressed to her front window. Zanthoula thinks there must be a mechanical bird in the saloon. But I have also detected a distinctive smell, which so excites my senses I cannot stay away.

One morning Zanthoula sees from billowing net curtains that the German couple have gone shopping, leaving *Enchanted April's* doors open to air the boat. Realising I will take this as an invitation to explore, she climbs aboard to close the yacht down, leaving a note to explain her reason for the intrusion. On glancing into the cabin, she sees a small brown bird with a splintered wing – a nightingale! So this is the Tweetie Pie to which I aim to play Sylvester! Later the couple call to thank Zanthoula, the gentleman confessing to have threatened me with a slipper, "You see," he explained contritely, "we thought he was a GREEK cat," (!!) adding, "He has more reason for his interest than you know, since, as well as an injured nightingale, we also care for a member of his natural prey, a mouse with a broken leg!

The day we leave Mitilini, Julia, growing more superstitious by the day, makes a big fuss. The date is Friday 13th, on which, she insists, it is unlucky to leave harbour. It is true that *Golden Prospect* failed to clear Mitilini until her third attempt because a plastic bag blocked her engine seacock. And she does run aground when we reached Scala Mistegnon, a harbour we have been assured offers plenty of depth. Julia then feels obliged to hand over a large bank note – a "whole week's housekeeping money" – as she ruefully puts it, to local fishermen in return for being pulled off a sandbank. "Well," she says, "it is all we had and I could hardly ask for change!") At least it makes *Golden Prospect* the most popular visiting yacht Scala Mistegnon has had for some time.

Circumstances improve after this and we dream-boat up the Muslim Channel to satisfy Zanthoula's desire to see the chapel of the Madonna of the Fishermen, Our Lady the Mermaid, at the entrance to Skala Sikinia. Sure enough, the *Παναγία της Γοργόνας* sees fit to acknowledge our salute so far as to waft us a favourable breeze. Unfortunately, when we reach the edge of her dominion, she runs out of puff, the breeze ending as abruptly as it began. This causes *Golden Prospect* to hit the doldrums all standing, with consequent damage to Gary's head by the boom, while Zanthoula catches her foot in my dirt tray. (She's always doing this. She never looks where she is putting her feet. The Captain says so too.) Everyone then gets cross when we tie up in Petra because all mooring rings are broken. It is not the luckiest of times. So perhaps Julia was right about Friday the Thirteenth?

However, Petra fulfils our dreams. None of us ever wish to leave the little settlement. Friendly fishermen, seeing our difficulty with tying up, press us to join them in their minute fishing harbour (a rare privilege) and keep us supplied with fresh fish, top quality καλαμάρες (squid), bass, sea bream and sardines, with plenty of small fry for me, in return for our fellowship and for Doctor Gary treating the hurt foot of an old reprobate of a fisherman we called "Compo" because he reminds my Pets of a TV character. We do even better when a hand-line fisherman offers to tutor Gary in eel fishing. Julia and Zanthoula are soon producing Greek-style bouillabaisse. As for me, I grow sleeker and fatter.

I also acquire two new playmates. One of them suffers a sad end, but the other becomes my best buddy. Early one morning Gary knocks on the hull to show us a mini-tortoise he has rescued from beneath the wheels of the fish lorry. Gary says he has "wound it up", for it pedals its legs in the air like a toy when he holds it on high. After that introduction, Tortie haunts us. We trail each other, me giving him a friendly pat on his back with my paw. But poor Tortie fails to stay away from the fish lorry and one day Gary discovers his crushed remains on the track.

My new sparring partner is a surprise Artemis held up her sleeve. With World Cup fever in the air, two Petra shopkeepers, butcher and baker (who know better) incense Julia by aiming a football at a bony little kitten as it seeks refuge amongst packing cases. One evening she expostulates as only Julia can. At this the butcher disappears into his shop and comes out carrying a sack, into which, without a word, scooping up the kitten, he drops it. Then, tying a knot in the top, he hands her the wriggling bundle. Having run out of steam, Julia is reduced to a stunned silence. "Is give you! Is present!" a woman in a doorway urges.

Thus "Soccer" joins our merry band. He tells me that he is of noble birth. (Of course, I don't believe a word of this.) He says his real name is Thucydides Zissimos or some such. But there can only be one name for him: "Soccer", which soon becomes "Socky". Cypriot worm pills and flea powders supplied by courtesy of *Cappelle*, sort him out, fleas proceeding to leave his person in such droves Julia tries to drown them in a bucket. Gary does his parental duty too, cutting a balloon fender in half and stuffing it with an old blanket to serve as Socky's basket. Socky is soon well set up.

I must say that at this point my emotions lead me to snub Julia. I have got so used to regarding her as my second mother that when she transfers her attentions to the welfare of another, it upsets my sensibilities. In the end my natural magnanimity leads me to be philosophical about this. As for Socky, he is nothing if not self-confident, verbalising enough to miaouw the legs off a millipede. **"WORRA! WORRA! WORRA!"** he growls horribly at any alien approach to his fish saucer. We cats are kept well provisioned by our fisherman friends, who bring us provender of such superior quality our human beans often persuade us to share it.

Socky and I are inseparable, racing after one another over our respective boats with the sound of stampeding elephants and playing

"I'm King of the Castle!" on top of the pile of burgundy fishing nets, two sets of black and white rumps quivering with excitement as we make ready to pounce. ("Gotcha!") Since Socky excels at street fighting, we enjoy some devilish spats. These consist of bouts of cuffing and buffeting, knock-downs, roll-overs, breakaways, frantic chases, ambushes, back-kick sparring in wrap-around hold, flying fur balls, bluffs, feints, duckings, stalkaways, even pretend grizzly endings with teeth buried in fur of opponent's throat. And always, of course, there are those nonchalant pauses for washing, designed to get the breath back and think through our next move.

I regret (albeit not deeply) to say that, once welded into a team, Socky and I get into the habit of ganging up on Gary, who becomes the unwitting butt of feline pranks. A tuft of Gary's hair sticking up above the coach roof, as he relaxes in the cockpit after the beans' regular afternoon swimming session, is enough to trigger me to launch an attack on Gary's head as if it were a furry animal. One afternoon when Gary sits chatting in his swim shorts holding a mug of scalding Winston Churchill (a popular brand of tea) between his thighs, Socky, with me in hot pursuit, plunges all too clumsily into Gary's mug, back legs first, scalding Gary in a sensitive area. This is hilarious for everyone except the victim!

The time comes at last to leave Petra. We would have liked to stay for ever and a day, or at least for rest of the summer, but my Pets remind themselves we are cruising, which involves not settling in one place. Our last expedition is to attend the Midsummer Festival of the Sardine in nearby Molivos where we gorge ourselves on barbecued sardines squeezed with lemon juice, slurp ice-creams, watch the fireworks and at last sail home by the light of the moon to the music of Beethoven played through speakers mounted on the coachroof.

Golden Prospect plans to travel south, we to make our way north. My last sight of Socky is perched on Julia's shoulder on the end of Petra pier, Gary beside them in his psychedelic tee-shirt. As the threesome wave goodbye, I call out, "Καλή επιτυχία! Στο καλο!" ("Good luck! May you go to the good!") especially for Socky. Julia makes him remember

Since Socky excels at street fighting, we enjoy
some devilish spats.

his manners and wave a paw. I am sure he carved out a great life for himself; he was that kind of guy.

My Pets survive on apple tea and peaches during our thirteen-hour sail to Mudhros on the island of Lemnos. A contrary current flowing out of the Dardenelles, with which I help the Captain cope, making for extra distance. Once in Mudhros I make a new acquaintance. When my Pets are invited to drinks on *Ros Arcan,* a converted fishing boat, I join them – I always keep an eye on my Pets; it is part of my duties – I admit to introducing myself to *Ros Arcan's* Ship's Cat, Muffin, a somewhat staid individual, rather pushily by chasing her round her own deck. Not very considerate you may say? At least it livens her up. She is inclined to avoid me afterwards, I must admit.

We dally in Mudhros longer than intended, for the Post Office is on strike and our Pets await mail. Mike, a new friend, skipper of *Runner Bean,* joins forces with the Captain to fix a defunct hydrant beside the quay, which then provides us with the luxury of fresh water. This shadeless island of Hephaestus, God of Fire and Industry, is otherwise virtually waterless – unless you strike lucky with the town well.

One drowsy afternoon I fall asleep under a tree where I encounter a warrior, who told me his name is Philoctetes. He says he has been abandoned on the island after being bitten by a snake on his way to Troy. Lemniot earth, an astringent clay also known as *terra sigillata,* is credited with curative powers, so Philoctetes sits there under a tree, poor man, with his foot buried in the earth, bored to death and glad of company. I wish him well, while remembering to avoid snakes in future.

One has some strange encounters on Greek islands. (Zanthoula has them too.) Once, when taking a nap in the bole of a tree I meet a pair of wood nymphs, a dryad and a hamadryad, who are arguing over status. The hamadryad, whose name is Chrysopeleia, declares she is the more important, because she has such a strong affinity with her tree that, if it dies, she dies with it. Anyway, she does not expect me to propitiate her, since Artemis, my creator, is a friend to all tree nymphs.

The islanders commiserate with us over the loss of the Football World

Cup in Sardinia to Germany. (I wonder what Socky thinks of this?) After the Captain stocks up with brass screws and other essentials at the hardware shop and we have picked up our letters, we organise a farewell barbecue at the head of the bay, which cuts so deep into the island it almost bisects it.

Our captains dive to dig in the anchors in the lee of a spit of land backed by a sand cliff. After setting up anchor lights, they leave me in charge while they row ashore with wine and barbecue fodder. I watch them carry benches from a chapel half-buried in the marram grass and stoop to gather driftwood for the fire. Then I fix my eyes on the glow of the flames far away on shore. I can smell the barbecue and hear them singing "Out of the swing, of the swing, of the sea" to the accompaniment of Mike's guitar.

I admit to being nervous about being left alone. When the moon rises, laying the Golden Way across the water once spread for the feet of Artemis, but latterly known as "Christ's Path", I try to commune with the goddess, hoping she is pleased with my development. As the air cools and a tickling breeze lifts the fur on the back of my neck, I wonder what I will do if the wind gets up. What if the anchor drags? Then the breeze gains strength and I think to warn the beach party. But they are too far away to hear me, heedlessly laughing and singing, failing to notice the swirling waves that are breaking on shore.

It was such a quiet evening that my Pets were careless enough to leave the sun awning and wind-scoop in place. The noise of flogging canvas, as well as the increasingly high whine of the wind unnerve me so much I wail out loud – "H-E-E-L-P! SAVE MEE PLEEZE! OWEE!" Soon I see movement ashore as my Pets and their friends awake in some alarm to reality, hastily stamping out the fire and rushing the borrowed benches back into the chapel. *Runner Bean's* anchor light has blown out – though you can still make out her silhouette against the sky. Unable to row against the strength of the wind, my Pets are the last to make it home. Mike, with his outboard engine, has to return to give them a tow, for by now the wind has grown too strong for even the Captain to row against.

My Pets are rightly chastened by their foolishness and by my distress, and do their best to comfort me. Our anchor holds, thank goodness, as by morning a gale-force north easterly is roaring straight at us across the isthmus. Mike's anemometer registers forty-two knots.

Protected from the sea's fetch by the isthmus, we stay put. The following day, the wind dropping, Mike's partner, Lindy-of-the-Long-Brown-Hair, rows over to tell us they intend to sail for the town of Myrina as soon as practicable, should we feel like going their way.

We battle to make passage as we sail the south coast of Lemnos in confused seas, coming face to face with a NEL lines ferry around Cape Tigani. Keep your wits about you, Wackster! I say to myself as, pitching and tossing, the Captain hanging onto the wheel, me calling "Port!" and "Starboard!" as appropriate, we slew *Cappelle* round to follow in the ferry's wake.

Mike is waiting on Myrina's quay to take our lines. He and Lindy are about to take their empties to fill with the Lemniot wine mentioned in Aristotle. This is on tap from barrels in the supermarket. But my Pets, clanking with bottles like disciples of Dionysius, take theirs straight to the wine factory to fill, since the supermarket barrels are most often empty.

ELEVEN

A Leap for Salvation

In which, fearing abduction, I take a flying leap.

We escape an explosion in a burger bar.

Cappelle is officially declared a "Friend of Myrina".

Centrally positioned on the island of Lemnos, Myrina is an international staging post for yachts cruising to and from the Black Sea. I am full of admiration for two magnificent Whitbread Swan 65s. (I wouldn't mind being Ship's Cat on a Whitbread!) I also like the γρίγρι, a boat with a fishing lantern and smaller boats strung out behind.

We enjoy watching the obese German couple on *True Love*. When they board their dinghy, *Tiny True Love*, its waterline plummets. One thing I do not welcome is Myrina's yearning for the glories of its naval past. At Church Parade the quay becomes unnervingly crowded with the marching boots of be-medalled veterans with scant regard for any soft-pawed pavement-sharer such as myself. In Myrina I live in dread of Big Boots.

My Pets are invited to take φλιτζανάκια (little cups) of Greek coffee by a neighbour, who wants to borrow a warp. Addressing me as "αγαπημενάκι μου" ("my little sweetheart") and declaring cats best on boats (hear, hear!), he relates the story of his poor little Maltese terrier, who broke her toe when she caught it in the scuppers. I also meet a dog whose yacht had been gale-bound. The poor chap was so seasick even his coat looked green.

On Friday the 13th of July, Zanthoula undergoes a strange encounter – or non-encounter, as you might say. Seeing, on her way to market, a previously unnoticed footpath, she swerves aside on impulse to follow it to the ruins of the Castle of Lemnos. Within the precincts, where tracks diverge, she takes the road less travelled, where she is confronted on the marble way with a freshly penned message on the step in front of her reading: *"Σε χαιρετώ παιδί του κάστρου – από το κάστρο σου"* ("I greet you, child of the castle, from your castle.") This is all very well, but the place is deserted. On the eve of our departure she returns to the castle and writes an answering message on the next step: *"Σ'αγαπώ το καστράκι μου – από την Ζανθούλα σου."* ("I love you my little castle, from your Zanthoula!") I wonder if that No One finds it?

As for me, I suffer an adventure that might well have ended badly. When a converted fishing boat draws in next to *Cappelle*, Sharp Eyes (me) at once spots a birdcage in the wheelhouse containing that essential concomitant of Greek family life, a canary. Needless to say, I cannot resist trespassing aboard to say "Hello". What I fail to realise is that the skipper is merely manoeuvring. Dissatisfied with his position and wishing to come in at a better angle, he pulls away. At this point I am convinced that it is the *Boomerang* situation all over again and that I have been press-ganged by Evil Doers. It is a fate to which death is infinitely preferable. There is no time to lose! The gangplank, not yet laid down for the convenience of disembarking passengers, is at vertical. Cat be nimble, cat be quick! I race up it.

The Captain's first sight of me is teetering with all four paws on the top rung of the upright gangplank. In a wild-eyed blur of panic, I am showing every intention of making a madcap death-defying leap into oblivion across the ever-widening expanse of harbour. It is now or never! As I launch myself off from my precarious perch – how glad I am to have practised the technique of the stretch-out from an aerodynamic back-feet-forward double bend, especially when performed with an aerial twist! – I am aware that crowds are gathering below yelling, "No! No! Wacky! Don't do it! Don't jump!" and that our gallant Captain has vaulted the cap-rail and cast-off our dinghy all in one bound. Too late! I am already swerving through space, paddling to adjust direction, tail outstretched, a squirrel cat, as I seek to wing it across the dark and dirty harbour. I know what it is like to be a bird in flight, except that a bird would be enjoying it and I, most certainly, am not. I also know that the touchdown, if I make it, will not be a well-sprung wooden deck, but an unforgiving concrete quay. In a four-point landing, I hit home. **OUCH**! The crowd cheers. But I do not wait to savour their acclamation. Never does a chap enter his own cabin so fast – and not through the port hole either. Am I thankful as I lie on the Captain's bunk on my back gasping for breath, all four sore paws held aloft to cool off.

Meanwhile I find myself a local hero. Fans gather. News of my exploit spreads. Gifts are laid at my door. A child brings Zanthoula a plate of sliced octopus "*για το ψιψινάκι σου*" ("for your little pussy cat"). A new friend, Matt, arriving with his wife for sundowners, calls out, "Shall we come aboard OR WOULD YOU RATHER WE STAND AND RECEIVE?" In one hand he is holding a box of chicken breasts (donor: unknown Greek), in the other, a party bag containing six individually foil-wrapped sardines (donor: girl on the caïque).

The following evening we are invited to drinks on *Clipper Ship Meredith* by Matt and his wife, who tells Zanthoula how much she "envies her her cat", her own Siamese having been killed in a road accident the day before they left for Greece. I must admit I was the first to notice a lobster under preparation in the galley. But before I can stretch out a larcenous paw, I am presented with a whole claw to myself.

I recover from my bad experience fast – who wouldn't with all that attention! But I vow to myself not to be quite so full of my own importance in future. However, it is worth remembering I am my own person now and that I no longer require a late pass. Hence, after we have dined out, my Pets leave me to my own devices. So I make a night of it, dodging bicycle wheels and hiding in the geranium beds. I nearly get into a spot of bother during our meal that evening by climbing the vine which branched above our table, instead of sitting quietly beneath it like a well-behaved

Ship's Cat should when taken out to dinner. The waiter, who has already brushed the tablecloth, is surprised to find it freshly covered in leaves and husks. Looking up, he spots two bright eyes (mine) staring down and hurries off, followed by Matt's wife, who suspects he has gone for a broom to dislodge me with its handle. "You mustn't," she tells him. "It's our cat." So my bacon is saved again.

On our last night in Myrina we pay a visit to a hamburger joint, which turns out to be dramatic. Our farewell salvo comes in the form of a blinding flash and an explosion that has us beating a retreat into the square. We are called back to find the cook, a dazed Greek Manuel with singed eyebrows, spread-eagled against the wall clutching a ladle. "Is orl right!" he gasps. "Is happen many time!"

Though we dally over two weeks in Myrina, when the Captain goes to collect our transit log and pay the harbour dues, the port policeman, roused at four in the morning, has a smile. A surprise is in store for the Captain. There is nothing to pay! *Cappelle* will always be exempt from dues, for the authorities have been pleased to grant her the official "Friend of Myrina" status (something akin to "Freedom of the City"). What an accolade! We are deeply honoured. (Note in diary: I mustn't let this go to my head.)

As we part company with Matt's clipper ship – we are to sail west for the Halkidiki, and Matt and his wife are to make their way east to Istanbul's new marina – Matt shouts, "And if you don't start fishing for that cat, we'll report you to the RSPCA!" (I intend to hold my Pets to this.)

Westbound with a favourable F 4/5 on the quarter, we encounter nothing more than a swathe of flotsam snaking in the current south of the island of Thassos. In the distance a silver tide of tuna fish splashes in the sun. Zanthoula takes off her clothes. (I do not think much of her in her skin, but she does enjoy sunshine all over.) My fur is not for stripping off. Sometimes on particularly hot days I wish it were.

TWELVE

Islanders Friendly and Unfriendly

In which we reach the Halkidiki.

My Pets take up fishing on Dhiaporos.

On Amouliani unfriendly natives block our anchor.

We are making for a three-pronged trident of land known as the Halkidiki, which juts out from the mainland into the upper reaches of the north-eastern Aegean just as if Neptune had plunged in his trident. (Perhaps he had!) Gradually there comes a thickening of the air on the forward horizon, which solidifies into the Holy Mountain dominating the tip of the Athos peninsula, the most northerly prong of the Halkidiki. (At this point Zanthoula puts her clothes on again. It is not seemly that the Mysterium Tremendum should be approached by a female bean, least of all an undressed one. We might be struck by lightning.)

As the afternoon light fades, encouraged by fishermen to whom we call out, "Ερχόμαστε απ᾽τη Μύρινα!" telling them where we are from, I guide us into the rock-girt harbour of Sikias on Sithonia, the central prong of Neptune's trident. Here the Captain drops anchor, setting a riding weight to hold us steady. The night wind brings fierce gusts accompanied by fitful lightning from the direction of Samothraki, making us glad not to have made Samothraki our destination, as at first intended. (The locals insisted the island was unsafe for a small boat in anything but the calmest of weather.)

When, in the early hours, a storm breaks, Zanthoula rushes to bring in the cockpit cushions. After the long, dry heat, the coachroof leaks. We put out buckets to catch drips, and I hide under the cabin table while my Pets crouch under the solid wooden overhangs above their berths. In the morning the sky is a washed-out blue and all is calm. But more καταγίδεσ (thunderstorms) are forecast. The bay is soon crammed with all manner of boats manned by exhausted and dishevelled crews. Our own in-harbour position is somewhat precarious because of the triple-wheeled freezer lorries that back down the mole. But the fishermen advise us not to leave yet. Best be safe, they say. "We will look after you and your Ship's Cat. "Σιγά! Σιγά!" ("Gently! Gently!"), they say, not seeming to resent *Cappelle* taking up space amid their fishing boats.

A pungent odour alerts me to an unfamiliar presence on a boat nearby. Once its crew departs I trespass aboard to investigate. The whiff draws me to an old motor tyre. What it contains is a sizeable turtle the fishermen have brought up in their nets.

One sleepy afternoon when Port Sikias is deserted and the weather seems calm, we worm *Cappelle* out of harbour, hand over hand, through networks of moorings, stern first, planning each move to port or starboard, while trying not to disturb or undo any moorings without refastening carefully, with me running from one side of the deck to the other miaowing directions – until, motoring in and out of gear, we find room to turn *Cappelle* around and float free. (How glad I am it isn't me in that motor tyre!)

We are making for the uninhabited desert island of Dhiaporos just off mainland Greece. A fisherman, seeing us leave Port Sikias, waves farewell. Pointing at the sky he calls, "Ο καλός καιρός!" ("Fine weather!") All the same, halfway along the coast of Sithonia, thunder reverberates along the hills and forked lighting strikes the sea ahead with the jag of a harpoon. It grows deathly dark and for a moment the waters turn black. Fearing the end of the world, I dive under the chart table, thinking the gods are after me and vowing to be a better cat in future. We are reefing down when ball lightning explodes. But then the storm passes over, leaving us almost, but not quite, sailing through a rainbow's arch. (So we have to wait for that crock of gold!)

By the time we reach our destination, the sky has cleared and soft zephyrs fan the air. As we drop anchor in Dhiaporos Bay, the late afternoon sun flares on a headland calvary, as if a votive light burns within. (Later the dip within really does shine within, for Zanthoula replenishes its lamp oil from the Coke bottle provided.) Dhiaporos Bay is wide and sandy. Realising that this is the perfect spot for my Pets to do their duty by me in inaugurating the rudimentary fishing tackle they acquired on my behalf in Myrina, I submit to the necessary trip in the dinghy.

I am uncomfortable on Dhiaporos's secret shore. It is too exposed. After crawling around on my belly, I slide nervously into the shadow of our upturned dinghy. Here I sprawl on the cool, damp sand, safe from the All-seeing Eye of the sun, longing to be back on my floating home. Now and again I pant a signal in case my Pets forget me – the gods forbid! But what really makes my heart miss a beat is when a darkly towering Behemoth steps out of the sea. I could have died of fright! It is evidently Polyphemos, the man-eating – and presumably cat-eating – Cyclops, who tried to sink Odysseus's ship with rocks. It becomes obvious to me he has a cave on Dhiaporos and that we are trespassing! He has gargantuan feet and an ungainly walk. He also sports a single funny eye –it is Polyphemus all right! Then I hear the Captain's voice and realise (Oh, the unspeakable relief.) that the ogre is the Captain himself in silhouette against the sun, galumphing out of the sea kitted out in his flippers and goggles. Such is my distress, my Pets take me home at once and do not persuade me ashore again.

Anyway, I have a great time at anchor when my Pets take to fishing from *Cappelle*. I am almost beside myself with the thrill of witnessing the new fishing tackle in action. With nylon threads wound round their fingers, baited fish hooks attached, my Pets yank out little fish after little fish, just the right size, as fast as they can swing their fishing lines. I quite lose my cool with excitement and have to be prevented from leaping at fishhooks. I just want the catch dropped into our blue bucket so that I can catch it all over again with my paw. This is the best game in the world! (If ever I see a blue bucket I still peer inside for fish. If the bucket has a lid, I push it off with my nose.) I always catch my own tea on Dhiaporos. There is nothing to rival self-caught fish for tea!

After about ten days at anchor we are running out of supplies, so sail across to Ormos Panagia on the mainland. Here the Captain gives Zanthoula instructions to hurry since the sea bottom is unsafe. *Cappelle* is already raising anchor for herself by the time she returns. Back on Dhiaporos, we edge into Porto Krifto, the Hidden Creek, a forest green tarn. There is an emergency that night when a swirling wind causes the anchor light to catch fire, but the Captain is quick to douse the flames with wet towels.

From Porto Krifto we sail on to Amouliani, a small island in the shadow of the Athos Peninsula whose sour-faced fishermen resent our approach, thinking, perhaps, we have come to take advantage of their precious water supply, while all we want is shelter for the night. Darkness begins with drunken youths on a ferry throwing chairs at one another and ends with me having a serious altercation with a boss-eyed tomcat, not to mention getting marooned on another boat after unwisely jumping into its hold. At four in the morning, after my Pets rescue me with the aid of a plank, we attempt to move out of harbour, but find a *caïque* has placed its anchor so precisely on top of our own the act can only have been deliberate. It takes super-human diving by the Captain, loops of rope and sustained heave-hoes from Zanthoula and me to drag *Cappelle*'s anchor out from beneath the imprisoning one.

THIRTEEN

The Forbidden Republic

In which we explore the coast of Athos and are officially
warned off.

I make friends in Porto Koufo.

We sail on to Porto Carras.

Our anchor freed at last, we cross the Gulf of the Holy Mountain and proceed down the coast of the Forbidden Republic marvelling at the sights it has to offer. What fun it must be to dance on the inebriated balconies of a fabulous Diaghilev-style monastery crouched beside the sea or, like Simonopetra, teeters over space on a dizzy cliff. It is notable that the Captain and I would be welcome should we apply to pay Athos a visit, but that Zanthoula would be barred just because she is a female.

With Zanthoula's hair neatly tucked into her yachting cap (we hope boyishly). we sail on, taking in the sights, while remembering to remain the regulatory 500 meters off shore, as prescribed for a private yacht with a woman on board. However, we are spotted. A state-of-the-art speed launch bearing the insignia of the ecclesiastical police force, the double-headed eagle, races towards us. Steering from a standing position, looking like Batman, is a smartly uniformed police officer in a flapping black cloak. Gesticulating angrily, he demands we stand out to sea. Time was when even female animals were barred from Athos, but lately a she cat, if a good mouser, and a she donkey, if a good bearer of burdens, has become acceptable. Obediently we turn away, knowing that, positioned at least half a mile offshore, we are already within our rights. Once down coast, we return to that distance and are not challenged again.

Where the sides of the Mysterium Tremendum rear steep-to comes an area known as the Ladder of Heaven. Its inhabitants are monks with heads for vertiginous heights, initially winched to their perpendicular eyries by pulley. (I should like to chase up to them with a fish to share.) Like all prudent sailors we cross ourselves beneath the Cave of the Wicked Dead beyond, before hoisting our blue cruising chute to say farewell to Athos. Poised on the taffrail, I make a striking figure. As we cross the Singitik Gulf a Hobicat puts out from the mainland to greet us, the couple on board calling, "You look so lovely out there, we've come to say 'Hi'."

Closing a cave-ridden headland, we make it into the Gulf of Kassandra to tie up in Porto Koufo (The Deaf Harbour), so sheltered that what the weather is like outside is anyone's guess. I at once hop onto the quay to make friends, escorting a likely-looking couple back to meet the family. The lady offers Zanthoula a lift in her car to the hilltop village of Sikia to buy stores, while her husband, knowing about the requirements of live-aboards, suggests ferrying the Captain to a garage to replenish our fuel canisters. The night is far from peaceful, for the quay is busy and decks of yachts have a magnetic attraction for carelessly tossed fish hooks and cigarette butts.

Later we help a Greek family tie up their new yacht, *Korina*. It is love at first sight for me and three-year-old Korina, the yacht's namesake. Like all Greek children, both boys and girls, Korina has been trained from an early age in the art of fishing and is already an expert. Every day parcels of fish are delivered for me. In Porto Koufo we know what it is to be spoilt, for Korina's mother, Xristina, brings us bowls of fruit from her garden in Thessaloniki. When, sometime later, en route for Porto Carras, we take the Boukadora, the favourable afternoon breeze. which blows up the coast of Sithonia, I am sad to leave Korina. When I

"Poised on the taffrail I cut a fine figure."

say, "Πρέπει να φύγα σήμερα!" ("I have to leave today!") she cries a bit. When I add, "Σ'αγαπώ!" ("I love you!") she cries a bit more. (One day she will read this diary!)

Porto Carras is an artificial yacht basin excavated from coastal flats. "A dream come true!" coos the brochure and we arrange to stay. We seem to be taking up residence at the Boat Show (whatever that is), says the Captain. In the mornings I awake to bird-song from the ornamental orange trees on the quayside. Then I devote my day to sitting beneath one, willing a bird to drop on my head. (A bird never does, but I have fun and catch a centipede.)

Beyond the quay a stone dyke supports a wild garden. The trouble with wild gardens is that they abound in ticks. I paw at the disgusting jelly-baby things that cling to my face until Zanthoula picks them off. I also have a hazardous encounter with a Doberman Pinscher on the loose. He scares me mightily and I flee up a tree. Now I never go there alone, but Zanthoula and I explore the flower-strewn hillsides together for orchids to put in her Greek vase. When I lose the Evil Eye off my collar in the wilderness one day the Captain is quick to fasten on a spare from our emergency supply. (I must never be without its protection.) Sometimes we visit Zanthoula's favourite swimming cove. On the bed of its sea garden, wavelets ripple the sand once swept into silver corrugations by the tidy Nereids, water nymphs, who tie the moon's rays into bundles to sweep the sea's sandy floor in radiating strokes.

Porto Carras encourages relaxation (and the writing of diaries). There is a disastrous occasion when I am possibly guilty of relaxing a bit too much. When Zanthoula is out shopping one day, I stretch out on the side deck as *Cappelle* sways gently in the sunshine, intending to fill my diary in. Although the atmosphere is undoubtedly soporific, I am wide-awake and engaged in creative thinking when somebody nudges me. I then find myself sliding, rear end up, into the sea. What a panic! I would never have been so stupid as to fall in without a push. Keeping my wits about me, though an inexperienced swimmer, I turn turtle under water as to the manner born and, making a supreme effort – death by drowning staring me in the face – bob up, gasping, to clamber onto our dinghy via its wooden backboard. From there, making use of a rope fender, I reach *Aegean Mistress*, our neighbour (leaving wet paw marks on her teak deck, as is reported). From thence I spring lightly onto the quay and run home to confront the Captain with a dripping apparition. He is dumbstruck. He hadn't even missed me. It is SO humiliating! I am too shocked to mew. Fortunately the precious diary has remained safe on deck during the emergency, but the Captain has a tale to tell Zanthoula when she gets back, which, I regret to report, he makes the most of.

The considered opinion of my Pets is that this unexpected ducking might have taught me a lesson about not indulging in the injudicious habit of staring down at fish, which (they wrongly imagine) led to me dozing off to join the aquatic band below. To my Pets this mishap (which was certainly NOT my fault) has its entertaining side. How sniggery of them! How unfair! Of course I forgive them. (I know which side my bread is buttered.) How could they be so unfeeling? It was Hermes, without a doubt, who flipped me overboard with a flick from one of his winged sandals. I know it. He always played the trickster in the Assembly of the Gods. If ever I get invited to their AGM on Mount Olympos, I intend to make a statement. At least my Pets have the common decency to avoid the touchy subject afterwards.

Aegean Mistress sails off to her winter quarters, while in Neas Marmaras inertia reigns. Stacks of firewood mount under the eaves. "Χειμώνας!" ("Winter!") says the old lady, padlocking her περίπτερο (kiosk) after scooping up the last of her peanuts to give Zanthoula. The days shorten. The temperature drops and drowsy wasps invade the cabin. (I know about wasps. Mess with them at your peril, especially those big yellow ones.) President Karamanlis's helicopter no longer lands at weekends and the marina empties for winter. It is very quiet with just us three. Only the occasional screech of a military jet reminds us of the war in the Gulf.

Most inconveniently, however, now it is out of season, there is nowhere to buy cat food. Not even cat biscuits would you believe? Zanthoula purchased tinned dog food. But it doesn't have the right vitamins for cats. The family, who run the shop which stocks the dog food, are worried about Zanthoula, thinking that, being but a poor boat person, she is buying the dog food to eat herself! However suitable supplies come my way via two German gentlemen, previous admirers of mine, who arrive to supervise the laying up of their boat. They are so kind as to bring me a gift box from Germany containing a splendid selection of cat food (including a packet of chopped bratwurst), for "the little cat who is like a dog". I am eternally grateful. The men say I remind them of A A Milne's James James Jonathan Jonathan Willoughby George Dupree, who told his mother she should "never go down to the end of the town" unless she went down with him. (This is because I play hide and seek with Zanthoula when she goes out shopping.)

Unbelievably, potable water has never been available at our luxury marina – just brackish stuff that no one will drink. My Pets purchase bottled water, with which plutocratic yacht owners fill their water tanks – an expensive habit. Once, after heavy rain, my Pets board a laid-up boat, taking a pan to scoop out the rain pooled in its tarpaulin to replenish our fresh water supply.

Last to vacate the marina is yachtsman Glyn, on his way to winter in Athens. Before the Captain leaves for a short break in London, Glyn invites him to accompany him when he takes his own water canisters to fill at a secret hydrant tucked away behind the third lamp-post from the end of the fishing quay across the bay.

Zanthoula cannot go to London because there is no one to look after me, and I can't go because of quarantine regulations. My Pets do try to find somewhere to lodge me, but the vet said no one would look after a cat "because cats run away". For a fee of five pounds a day there is an offer to imprison me in an old airport building and throw me scraps – an idea my Pets reject out of hand, of course. Then the girl at the airport begs the Captain, with tears in her eyes, not to send me to kennels in Thessaloniki, saying conditions are so bad there that, on visiting her friend's little dog, "When I see him, I cry!"

FOURTEEN

Land Base with Resident Witch

In which the Captain and I move to Neas Marmaras.

We escape the clutches of a Mad Woman.

As we leave Porto Carras we are befriended by pirates.

When the season ends we are made especially welcome in the village because of our change of status from summertime visitors to sharers of winter. Mothers sitting on kitchen chairs outside their doors send toddlers learning to walk to Zanthoula for her to turn around and direct staggering back to their mothers. The green grocer stuffs her basket with new winter vegetables for "Ὄχι δράχμες!" ("No money!") as he puts it. And in the street market, fruit sellers heap her shopping basket with free tomatoes, adding a pomegranate or two as a treat. Accepted by the community, we live well.

Then it is the Captain's turn to stay behind, while Zanthoula keeps a dental appointment in London. When her return is delayed, she despatches us a "special delivery" parcel of goodies containing a fan-heater, books, puzzles, cat treats, a cake and chocolates. It never arrives! After a trace is put out by the GPO in London, the parcel is discovered lurking in a sorting office in Thessaloniki, going nowhere. It must be fetched.

Across the water as the sun declines, the peninsula of Kassandra lies soot black against a red-hot poker sky. The temperature drops. The

Little Summer of St Demetrios ends. There will be no more swimming in the Garden of Thalassinous Delights. Heavy rain continues. The river bursts its banks to dissect the beach and join the sea in an ever-widening stream. Except via a circuitous route inland over a road bridge and along the main road, the Captain and I are cut off from the village. After a further storm, he is forced to wade thigh-high to make a telephone call, at which point he decides it is time to seek us accommodation in Neas Marmaras while awaiting Zanthoula's return. He takes up the first offer, a self-contained flat over a garage, which belongs to a Greek, whose Manchester-born wife welcomes him with open arms, saying he is an answer to her prayers for he solves a problem, since she wishes to spend Christmas in England with her family, but is anxious the property should not be left unattended.

(All the same my instinct tells me there is something weird about her.) We arrange to move in at a nominal rent, the Captain as caretaker, until such time as the weather improves and we can return to our boat. There is a bicycle for the Captain's use, "if he can mend it", we are told. (You can say that again, since it is minus its rear wheel!)

The apartment is very clean, though sparsely furnished, Mrs Koutanou promising to curtain the French window. The Captain loses no time in hiring a taxi and moving us in together with our creature comforts, my blue bowl, our duvets and soft furnishings, plus radio, kettle and pressure cooker. When we arrive we find the property already empty and our window still uncurtained.

Shortly afterwards the temperature falls to ten degrees below and blizzards start. I soon get my bearings, climbing down from our balcony to cross the snowy track to the cliff top and returning to feed from my blue bowl before snuggling between duvets. My greatest mistake is to fall into a bucket of slaked lime while exploring outbuildings. The Captain does his best to scrape the stuff off, but I admit to looking piebald for a while.

I never do take to our landlady on her return. The funny look in her eyes has grown more apparent. Greek neighbours, who appear concerned for the Captain's welfare, invite him to their New Year party. Here they tell him how Mrs Koutanou sets off a hooter alarm on her roof whenever their little dog barks, and about her habit of leaving her washing machine permanently switched on and of using the vacuum cleaner all night. I stay well out of her clutches, noticing how careful she is to avoid Zanthoula on my Pet's return. Zanthoula does not unpack.

As soon as the weather improves the Captain goes to settle up, leaving Zanthoula and me to finish cleaning, clearing and packing. What next assails our ears is a violent altercation. We can hear the Greek demanding high season rental, plus redecoration of the entire apartment at overtime rates, the dry-cleaning of the horse blankets which had never been removed from the wardrobe, plus extras, which laughably include "hire of bicycle". Meanwhile a deranged Mrs Koutanou screamed obscenities. If strong language in Greek makes your ears pop, it could not compete with the Manchester version. I set about sharpening my claws in case the Captain should need my support. That witch would not like ME on her back!

The Captain threatened to call the police, at which the Greek snorts, saying there are no police, since the police station is closed out of season. Citing Greek greed and Mancunian insanity, anxious to get away and using up three of our precious Euro cheques, the Captain at last pays triple what could reasonably have been expected, though far from the preposterous sums demanded. Not waiting to put me in my holdall, Zanthoula sweeps me into her arms and we descend to a waiting taxi, where the driver, who gives the impression of having seen it all before, sits in silence. As we leave, pots and pans are whistling through the window and a mad woman screaming "Filthy bastards!" is hammering on the wall. We learn the couple had attempted to emigrate to Australia, but that Mrs Koutanou's behaviour on arrival had been so extreme she was immediately sectioned and deported.

At the sight of yacht masts I scrabble at the taxi window to get out. None of us, whatever the hardship to come, had ever been so glad to be back on *Cappelle*. Soon I am running about trilling at the rediscovery of all I know while my Pets laugh with relief and collapse with a stiff drink.

The deserted marina is our home now and we make the most of it. With the river still swollen, the Captain maps out a middle-distance approach to Neas Marmaras along the riverbank as far as the road bridge, before joining a cut-back to the beach past the remains of a tuna-smoking factory. Soon the estuary drains enough to ford with caution. With the waters constantly changing course, Zanthoula crosses holding the shopping on her head. Once she steps in quick sand and is forced to lie flat to extricate herself. She does long for a donkey, she says, such as the one she feeds with an apple. Needless to say, I stay well away from the river.

It becomes clear the marina is in limbo. The manager, the deceased owner's friend, has walked out, taking all staff and documents with him. Boats may now come and go as they please, without payment. Law suits are pending. My Pets keep busy with odd jobs, reading books and listening to the BBC World Service. Somehow we all enjoy life, especially after the Captain discovers a constant flow of hot water issuing from broken piping in an outbuilding. The fact that the rain pours down non-stop means we have fresh drinking water too!

In Neas Marmaras the villagers' smiles turn into Easter Greetings. The Papa in his tall hat strokes me kindly and pats Zanthoula on the head when she acknowledges his Easter greeting in the correct idiom answering, "Αληθώς ανέστη!" …"He is risen indeed!" to his "Χριστός ανέστη!" …"Christ is risen!" Lilac and hottentot fig burst into flower at the back of the beach. The Greeks have a saying that "Pouring Easter weather brings Happiness and Plenty both together". So, according to tradition, we are in for a fine summer. It is time to be on our way.

With persistence, the Captain obtains a new engine battery. But on the day we plan departure we awake to an adverse change in the weather as the marina fills with fishing boats seeking shelter from a storm. As often, when the weather is bad, the forecaster fails to turn up at the radio station. It is not until a few days later, on the back of the storm, that we move out of Porto Carras. As we sail away, Zanthoula tosses into harbour

our latest bunch of ribbon-tied orchids in votive offering to Aphrodite Euploia, goddess of Fair Sailing.

Our first stop is at Glyn's water hydrant. From here we intend to make the short passage down Gulf to Porto Koufo where, when assured of a favourable wind, we will head off for Myrina again, our nearest port of exit from Greek waters. Though caïques block our way, a fishing smack crewed by pirates, swarthy giants with red bandanas and gold teeth, pulls us in amongst them. I find it most exciting that the Pirate Captain really does wear a gold hoop earring! The pirates greet me with friendly words and want me to sign on as a Pirate cat, an offer I do not accept, but which pleases me mightily because I am feeling sore about being torn from the Enchanted Place. (I also have a secret yen to fly the Jolly Roger!) The pirates want to know what my Pets with Ship's Cat and Red Ensign are doing out and about so early in the year. When we tell them we are on our way to Myrina they bravo!

While the water hose is fitted, Zanthoula runs up the hill to the baker. When she gets back the grimy fingers of a ringleted Captain Hook hold out to her a patched colander of fresh sardines. Zanthoula proffers coins, but Captain Hook will have none of them. That night Zanthoula cooks us such a succulent dishful of pirate-caught sardines it almost makes up to me for the loss of the Enchanted Place. No meal could be finer. (My Pets eat theirs with hunks of fresh-baked Neas Marmaras bread, all washed down with Athos wine.)

Porto Koufo, devoid of yachts but with fishing boats belching fumes as they reload their nets, is unrecognisable out of season. But with the departure of the fishing fleet, peace is restored but not for long. Soon the first fleet returns and the loading of fish lorries starts up again inches from our noses. From midnight to 2 a.m. there is a lull and then the activity is renewed with the arrival of the second fleet. Boats queue up, while a shuttle service of lorries hoots its way down from the road above before backing along the mole. Men shout, engines roar, doors slam. With a vision of the biscuits waiting for me in my blue bowl, I am glad to make it home.

The following day brings a wet mist and an increasingly unfavourable wind. A fisherman approaches the Captain, wagging his finger, to say, "No you go! You stay Porto Koufo!" which is nice of him, since we are out of place taking up room amid so much industry. On the third morning the wind changes and we set sail. We are in for a big send-off when we meet Captain Hook and his merry men coming in. They salute us with high fives while I jump up the mast to wave a paw. "Καλό ταχίδι!"("Good journey!") they call.

Twelve hours later a patrol boat from Myrina, recognising *Cappelle*, puts out to escort us into harbour, indicating to us to tie up against a disused caïque, since the fishing fleet is due. *Cappelle* is the third boat out from the quay, so I am careful to practise going back and forth to orientate myself before making my final departure. Then, after a quick brush-up of my cognitive map, I set off to enjoy a night's clubbing in familiar territory.

The islanders boast their climate is "just like England" for in Myrina rain has scarce ceased for a month. When we check out there are no dues to pay. *Cappelle* will forever be a "Friend of Myrina".

FIFTEEN

Landfall in Turkey

In which we run hard aground in the Muslim Channel.

We tie up in Turkey.

Back on Lesbos I react badly to an injection and am feared run over.

We drop anchor on Psara.

The stars are peeping when, seen off by cormorants, we head east for the Muslim Channel. Perhaps it is not sensible to plan to cross the shipping lanes of the Dardanelles during the hours of darkness. But, on the other hand, it is prudent to make landfall on an unfamiliar stretch of the Turkish coast in daylight.

Yet again my night sight proves its worth. One boat appears to have a slow-burning brazier on deck, but it quickly metamorphoses into a rising copper moon. Sighting the lights of the coast of Asia Minor, I make warning noises. Then Zanthoula goes off watch, leaving me to guide the Captain through some complicated manoeuvres. Beating into tossing seas, we attempt to force our way into the Muslim Channel, while avoiding semi-submerged rocks on the Turkish side. Aiming for what he thinks is a red navigation light on Cape Molivos, I alert him to the fact that it is the port light of a fishing boat. (Neither skipper relished the ensuing close encounter.)

It takes all the Captain's strength to bring *Cappelle* between Baba Burun, notorious for gusts, and Cape Molivos in a head-sea roughened by a Poyraz, a cold and blistering north-easterly wind prevalent in the area at this time of year. There are still more capes and islands to negotiate before we pick up a landmark.

Worse comes later when the channel through the Ayvalik archipelago opens up, or rather fails to open up. (We should have consulted the Admiralty Chart – always more accurate than the local Pilot.) Quite without warning, the dreaded happens and we run hard aground under full sail in the middle of nowhere. Revving the engine in reverse, rocking the hull and tugging the yacht with the dinghy, the classic remedies are all of no avail. I long for a team of dolphins under harness to come to our rescue – descendants of Pausanias's celebrated dolphin from nearby Porsolene, perhaps, who once saved the life of a boy.

The area is unfrequented but, after I wing an urgent appeal to Aphrodite Euploia, there appears a speed boat driven by German resident, Otto (unusually late back from a fishing trip, he tells us). Making strenuous efforts to drag us out of the mud with his powerful engine, Otto at last succeeds. It is a notorious spot for running aground, he says. Then, with repairs apparently necessary to our bilge pump, which had suffered mysteriously in the grounding, we clank ignominiously up the buoyed channel to Ayvalik.

My "Merhaba!" ("Hello!") in Ayvalik is acknowledged in a friendly manner and I am quick to pick up the standard Turkish politesses. We revel in a new diet. My Pets drink apple tea and gorge themselves on the fat local olives and strawberries just come into season. Sardines make a splendid supper. The Captain devises a contraption to keep the fish cool by rigging up a double plastic bag system to dangle over *Cappelle*'s side. The bigger fish from the market are secured in the inner bag, but the outer bag, which the Captain fills with water, for some reason attracts swarms of small fry. Tipped into a washing up bowl these make fine sport for me! From then on I glory in the catch and the feasting, even when it means getting drenched. On a night out, however, I am incautious

So what's this new place? Ayvalik is my first experience
of the Islamic umbrella.

enough to lick the salt slabs in the fish market, which produces such a raging thirst I rampage back to *Cappelle* in the early hours, knocking over the milk jug (not a popular move) to slurp a draught of washing-up water.

Ayvalik is my first experience of the Islamic umbrella. At first I run home when the Muezzin sounds, convinced that Allah Himself is after me, but the call to prayer soon forms a pattern in my life. I am made much of by many. My only problem is to acquire a deadly enemy, a runny-membraned tomcat. We call him Saddam because he is Terror Incarnate! He is also a Social Stink Bomb, whose rank stench makes me feel faint. When Saddam invades our sovereign territory, my teeth chatter. My Pets once catch him in broad daylight standing foursquare over poor me pinned on my back on my own deck. He even commits the ultimate insult of defecating in our cockpit. A high pressure hose means nothing where he is concerned. The Captain then resorts to a dastardly weapon called a catapult (presumably invented for the protection of cats). But even if he does catch Saddam square on his marmalade backside we are never entirely free of him popping up like Beelzebub, sizzling for a fight and leaving his stink behind. My ardent prayer is that he and Lord Byron of Cyprus meet up one day – they'd make a splendid pair.

All too soon it is time for the Turks to bid us a regretful "Güle güle" ("Go smiling! Go smiling!") and for us to reply, "Allahaismarladik!" ("May God stay with you!") as we set off for the Cycladic Islands.

We re-enter Greece by way of Mitilini, where, to our surprise, we pick up a greeting, via the BBC World Service. from Julia and Gary who are sitting under a tree in a rain forest in Borneo. "I Wanna Break Free" by Queen is played on their behalf.

My problem with the infective Saddam reminds Zanthoula my booster shot is due, so she hauls me off to the local small animals vet, who is delighted to make my acquaintance when he finds I have been a patient of his friend of student days, Adrianos of Rhodes. (This is what human beans mean when they talk about "small world". It seems a very big world to me and gets bigger every day.) A short while later I have a violent reaction to the shot and became dreadfully poorly, leading to Zanthoula bursting in on the vet when he is operating on a dog. Filling a hypodermic, he sends her scampering back to *Cappelle* to administer the antidote.

In a few days I recover, but then my energy levels nearly prove my undoing. The weather worsens. When gale force winds bring a heavy swell through the harbour entrance, my Pets are obliged to spend the night in the cockpit keeping an eye on the situation, the engine ticking in reverse to hold *Cappelle* off the quay. In a dawn lull we make haste to move over to the more sheltered town quay. Our new berth also has its dangers, since the waterfront is a through-route for traffic. Although Zanthoula does her best to divert my attention when she goes shopping one evening, I foolishly follow her across the road. The traffic is scarier than I had bargained for, so I squeeze under the newspaper kiosk opposite the boat, too frightened to move. My Pets are terribly upset when they discover me missing, especially when a fisherman tells them he has seen me follow Zanthoula across the road. They search and search, but only when the circulation quietens down around midnight do I venture home. Poor Zanthoula, who feared the worst, dries her tears on my fur.

After a brief stopover in Plomari, where we experience the notorious "Plomari swell" (full responsibility for which the Port Police place on Iraqi oil fires) we sail for Psara, a tiny, mid-Aegean island ten miles off Chios, a favourite of small boat sailors. Odysseus, homeward bound from the Trojan War, kept Psara to port, but we enter harbour, where a Papa in a tall hat and greenish-black soutane greets us, anxious for news of the world outside. "Εχουμε ησυχία," ("No news. All is well,") we tell him.

Psara has been legendary from the time of Ceres, who reached it in her search for her daughter, Persephone. A widow, seeing her distress, leaned out of a window to hand her a bowl of honey-water sprinkled with barley, but the widow's runny-nosed, razor-headed little boy cheeked Ceres, not knowing her to be a goddess, at which she changed him into a gecko. The razor-headed little lad's descendants still populate Psara! I know because I play with them. I also make friends with a white egret, while Zanthoula chats to a Great White Pelican who fixes her with his albino eye.

SIXTEEN

The Central Islands

In which we explore the Cyclades.
We back-track to Amorgos.
We sail west for Pholegandros.

Then comes the time to make the sea crossing to the Cycladic islands over what Odysseus called that "weary stretch of water". The sea is a millpond. Off watch for once, I sleep all day, curled round like a doughnut in the forepeak, waking only for the docking process on the far side of the island of Andros after the sea-crossing is over. (The Captain relies on me to organize docking. Then I hand over to him and he thinks he's done it all himself.)

There is little current running in the Doro Channel, but the haul to the deep inlet of Gavrion beyond is long drawn out. At least we don't have to sacrifice a bull's thigh, as did Odysseus. (The gods got the best cuts and the islanders the rest.) Duty done, I put my front paws on the cockpit rail and stand tall to give this new port of call the once over. I at once spot hand-line fishing in progress. For me, this is the best spectator sport in the world, with a prize at the end, if you play your cards right.

We were lucky with the crossing. Next day the winds are so strong even the big ferries with their powerful twin-screw engines are cancelled. A fishing boat stands off while its skipper waits for us to untie our extra spring lines to let it in. Then he insists we re-tie our lines behind him to keep us all secure. (He throws me a fish.)

It is evident that water in the Cyclades is a platinum resource, village taps usually cough only spiders and dribbles. Yachtsmen beg and borrow fresh water wherever they can. Some even steal it, or spend a fortune buying it for washing as well as drinking. (There's nothing like a good lick to get you clean, I say. And what's wrong with sea water for washing human beans and boiling potatoes?) One yachtsman we know habitually wears a backpack in which he keeps a water jar, which he replenishes whenever he gets the chance.

In the next lull we leave for Tinos, Andros's sister island, divided from it by the Steno Strait. As we pass the opening, a swordfish rockets into the air, so close to our bows it took my breath away. (I am sure I hear it cry "Excalibur!") We soon spot the foam-white town of Tinos scintillating at the edge of the sea like a wedding cake. The presence of a water hydrant on its waterfront means we have reached our Eldorado, for Tinos boasts the sweetest water in the islands. Our hopes are dashed, however, with a notice that Tiniot water is "NOT AVAILABLE TO YACHTS". Moreover, on the Captain prizing up a hydrant cover beneath an exquisite white marble pediment carved with fishes and sailing ships, all it produces is a scream from Zanthoula as massed cockroaches erupt. (Zanthoula is not keen on cockroaches and I only like them to tease people with. Give me a gecko anytime!)

In Tinos I temporarily acquire a new name. The Captain sometimes calls me "Wackster", which the people on a neighbouring yacht mishear for "Webster", believing I am named after P G Wodehouse's cat of that ilk. My Pets are too polite to disabuse them and so, briefly, I become "Webster". (Fine by me, as long as they feed me. I think to myself. Moreover, the name does have a certain ring.)

I don't think it is my new name that does it, but the next thing I do is, as near-as-ninepence, get run over. After standing on the coach roof watching a priest carried by on a palanquin, the Captain, wondering where I have got to one evening, summons me. As always, at the sound of my Captain's voice, I am all attention, for when he wants me, he really wants me. But this dash across the road, looking neither right nor left, had me almost under the wheels of a speeding car. (It must be Artemis, believing I still have work to do, who saves me from losing all the lives I have left.) Whew! What a close shave! My Pets come over all trembly and I learn a lesson. After this the Captain vows to leave me to my own devices in future. From then on I am very careful how I cross the waterfront to join the nightlife the other side. On Tinos I become an habitué of some excellent establishments and am finding myself now quite well known in the islands. People ask after me. In fact I am spoken of as the most travelled cat in the Aegean.)

Caught in the wind triangle of Tinos, Mykonos and Delos, we experience siege conditions as the meltemi roars in, blowing away the atmosphere to leave wind-laundered air in which colour shimmers and white dazzles the eye. On Tinos we watch huge ferries winched to safety out of spume-lashed seas and distressed VIP passengers landed. It feels cosy to be weather-bound on such an island.

I introduce myself to the local pelican, a Tinos mascot, who hangs out near the supermarket. (Sometimes he goes inside and patrols the aisles, he says.) He is old and smelly and can be irritable, but is an interesting character. Lawsuits on his behalf are not unknown. Some believe he lives forever or, as cynics suggest, is swapped at the critical moment for a younger model.

As soon as the meltemi shows signs of abating, we are off to Delos, the focus of the pagan world. I long to visit this island because it claims the birth of Apollo the Sun God, Artemis, my creator, being his twin sister. (Once I catch the twinkle of her silver sandals as she runs lightly across the bed of the Sacred Lake towards the palm tree planted in her brother's memory.) We cannot stay long, however, for a curfew falls mid-afternoon, by which time, due to an increase in theft and vandalism, all yachts must clear. After exploring the Terrace of the Lions and sampling the tinkling water in the fountain courts of the peristyle houses on the slopes we set off to Mykonos, *Cappelle* the first private yacht to reach the island after the meltemi. Mykonos with its hill-top windmills and contour-hugging alleyways, is real cat country. Off the south coast my Pets fish for me.

On the island of Paros, I am introduced to a red-haired Scots girl, who lives in a but-and-ben with a crooked stair where she sells herbs and potions for "headaches and madness". She begs me to stay, but I have other plans. Anyway, I am settled in my career. One thing which haunts me is a notice pinned to a door down cellar steps reading: "I give babies pussy cat miaowing Greek." Before we leave Paros we are all relieved to see the four kittens on offer reduced to one.

Our next stop tests my professional skills to the full. Leaving Paros just as the Cycladic dawn is breaking, we enter the "Fourteen-foot Passage" (as marked on the Admiralty Chart) leading to the island of Ios. The passage has silted considerably since Commander Graves's of the Royal Navy's day and is not to be attempted by any yacht of deep draught. *Cappelle* might just make it, islanders advise, if we conduct ourselves with extreme caution. Zanthoula mans the echo sounder (with which she irritates the Captain by calling it "the depth charger") while I dash port and starboard to check the depth over the side, the Captain steering according to my directions. We line up with the light on Salango, a summer isle named from the cry of the herdsmen, and then inch our way past the Islands of the Rapids, where the echo sounder registers less than ten feet. Safely past this hazard, by midday we have sighted Dhiakoft (Twin Blade Islet), our landmark for Ios, to complete the twenty-six mile passage.

Ios, island of the goddess Io, really is my cup of tea, especially its enclosed harbour with raised flower beds. (The Captain writes "Good cat country" in the log book.) A voice calls, "Almost a year ago today!" and there is Ros Arcan last met on Lemnos, cat Muffin still a member of crew. (She blinks a bit when she sees me!) We are in Ios because it is the recommended safe harbour to leave a boat while its crew visit Santorini, an anything-but-safe island for a yacht when tied to its mooring buoy, a tatting reel of warps in the thousand-foot depths of the caldera.

My Pets do not allow me ashore on the Burnt Islands which lie at the centre of the Caldera. Here volcanic activity still shows in flickers of blue flame. (If I venture ashore I might cut my paws on the sharply glittering black scoriae, or singe my tail, but I do sniff the fiery fumes, which make me sneeze.) There are rumours of a large and bold breed of rat on the Burnt Islands, which would not hesitate to board a yacht even in broad daylight. The very idea of such intrusion makes my whiskers bristle.

We plan to be on our way west. That is to say until Zanthoula begs to turn back towards Turkey to explore the beautiful outrigger island of Amorgos she has had recommended. On the morning of departure I present my Pets with a giant moth, which Zanthoula dispatches with the fish slice.) At first *Cappelle* yaws in the decayed swell of a southerly, which levels out when we change course onto a dead run for Amorgos. Once in harbour my Pets combine breakfast and lunch while I attend photo calls.

On Amorgos the story is told of a French Ship's Cat, Jean Luc, who fell asleep on a fishing boat and disappeared for weeks. Eventually he was returned to the island after his inadvertent holiday. Here the butcher looked after him until his frantic owners flew out from Paris to collect him. Hey, Jean Luc! What an expensive escapade that turned out to be!

The cliff-top monastery of Khozoviotissa hangs over the sea gleaming white like a dragon's egg. Zanthoula, who is wearing trousers (wide-legged silk ones, which she thought suitable), is disconcerted to find a notice at the monastery gates declaring, "NO WOMEN IN TROUSERS". But the Abbot and Beadle relent after they make her climb steps in front of them so they can scrutinise her modesty. I stay outside meanwhile, in the garden, in conversation with the monastery's black kitten, until called in to be presented to the Abbot, who wishes to meet me since he is impressed by my official position and amazed that the three of us plan to sail home to England. He hastens to show My Pets a celebrated painting known as the Deesis of Gennedios. Dating from 1619, it commemorates a storm in the dangerous seas between the islands of Amorgos and Paros. This is the storm that brought about the cessation of the age-old close relationship between these islands.

Before leaving Amorgos, I award myself a grand night out of Amorghian adventure in the marshlands, with scratches on my nose to show for it. It nearly makes me late for departure and brought Jean-Luc's escapade to my Pets' minds. When the gravity swell dies, we sail on a beam reach in the lee of the Agrilios Islets. Here Theseus had abandoned Ariadne, who went to live among the stars as the Corona Borealis. We are without charts for this area, so, keeping an eye out for hidden reefs while cumulus clouds build over the silent sands of Naxos, I seek out an anchorage where I hope we may safely spend the night.

Next day the true light of Apollo shines. With our senses quickened, we can pick out every detail on the string of islets that lie between Sikinos and Pholegandros. Port Karavostasi ("Port Shipwreck"), our intended destination on Pholegandros, lies behind a wickedly arthritic arm of reef. All my skills are called into play until we are safe and sound inside Karavostasi's Bristol-blue depths. I am much flattered when a yachtswoman calls out, "How I wish we had HIM to help." Then she goes on, "Don't you ever worry about him?" I am relieved to hear Zanthoula tell her that she and the Captain count on my ability to look after myself, as well as keep an eye on their welfare.

SEVENTEEN

Land of Peel Towers

We round Cape Malea to Gytheion.
We sail the Deep Mani to enter a pirate redoubt.

Pholegandros is compact enough for us all to get to know. A cat could spend a lifetime on this delightful island. The walls of its citadel enclose a trim mediaeval housing estate full of narrow passages giving off scrumptious mousy smells. This is excellent from my point of view, for no one has ever heard of tinned cat food on Pholegandros. Quite rightly, you are expected to catch your own tea.

As we all stand together on the dizzy rim of the acropolis, at its foot a seething cauldron of white water stretching northwards, the meltemi forces our breath back. Known locally as the "Καμπάνατος", its name stems from the deep boom of church bells, which ring for themselves as the wind strengthens. With NW Force 6 increasing from strong to high, sea rough, it looks as though the Καμπάνατος is gaining ascendancy. But, on due assessment, if we gamble on sailing south west, the Captain reckons we shall enter quieter conditions, since to the south the blow is predicted to moderate.

Circling in harbour, we make all secure and raise sail. The confused seas outside around Cape Katergo give problems, but after an hour or so the Captain and I are able to settle *Cappelle* on course to make direct passage west, across the Mirtoan Sea, under full main and sail on a beam reach – me, whenever I have a moment, gobbling a mouthful of a mouth-watering fricassee of chicken chopped in sardines specially prepared for me by Zanthoula to keep my strength up.

Above us and below streams the shimmering belt of the Milky Way (above in reality, below in reflection). Sometimes I sight Artemis slaloming down an arrow of moonlight while galloping her silver chariot along the Way. Passing south of Milos we close bun-shaped Paximadhi Islet in order to steer clear of the Ananes (Pineapple Islands), whose Group Flashing Light is out of order.

Dawn brings a stunning revelation. Five miles ahead in warm early light rears the Caput Formidatum Maleum – Cape Malea in all its glory. The Captain shouts for Zanthoula (off watch and fast asleep) to join us to share the moment. Ahead of us the Peloponnesus ends in a giant dinosaur's foot, mammoth grey, steep-to and six miles wide. With Zanthoula zombified by the view, the Captain and I keep a sharp look-out, since there is no separation zone. Ships troop down the nearside coast of the Peloponnese towards the important shipping lane between the island of Kithera and the mainland. Black squalls off the heights ruffle the water as we set our course our under full sail beneath Cape Malea. *Cappelle*, slotting into the groove, flies like a bird, her wheel answering to the Captain's finger-touch. An eyrie on the heights shows where an anchorite once lived – perhaps lives there still? If so, I wonder if he has a cat. I should like to be that cat – temporarily, of course, to bear witness to *Cappelle*'s triumphant sail.

Before entering the Malea Channel, the Captain makes a half-hearted remark about getting a reef in. But, spirits soaring, none of us have any truck with cowardice. Then, after we pass Cape Zovolo gusts of Force 7 slam us on the nose. "Too much sail!" yells the Captain. In sight of Elaphonisos (Deer Island), Nemesis waits to punish vainglory with the full force of a blistering north easterly out of Vatika Bay. The Captain fights the helm in an experience that parallels that of Odysseus, "I might have made it safely home, but, as I come round Malea, the current takes me out to sea, and from the north a fresh gale drives us on past Kithera."

"We've GOT to get a reef in!" hollers the Captain, battered by the elements. Zanthoula, grabbing the helm, exerts all her strength to head us into wind and hold us there, no mean task. Once she succeeds in screwing *Cappelle* around, she and I both try to fix our streaming eyes on the tell-tales at the top of the mainsail to make sure we hold steady facing the Donkey's Jaws (an old name for Deer Island) while the Captain winches in the genoa and recovers the log. This is just before a giant wave hits us. Seeing me about to take air, Zanthoula momentarily lets go of the wheel to hook me with her foot and clamp me under her arm before flinging me unceremoniously into the cabin. What treatment. After all my efforts. Though, as Zanthoula explains later, the slippery side deck I was leaping for might well have been my undoing. *"Surrexit, Alleluia,* Wackster!" I think. Anyway, I see fit to forgive her. My Pet means well.

Beyond the Malea Gate we enter a new dimension. I understand the meaning of the sailors' saying, "Round Malea forget your native land" – not that I ever would forget mine – but I appreciate the respect sailors have for Malea, which collects depressions like a philatelist collects stamps.

Sorted, with one reef in the main and half a genoa, we sail west across the Gulf of Lakonika, which lies between the heavily indented arms of Greece's most redoubtable mountain ranges, on one side the High Taigetos and, on the other, the Parnon Range. We are not sure as to our best landfall. We could take advantage of the favourable winds to reach Porto Kaio, a pirate redoubt on the far side of the Gulf. It affords good shelter, its disadvantage being that it offers no supplies, no water and no fuel, and we are already short of the latter, since there has been no chance of a fuel refill since leaving Paros.

At the head of the Gulf, however, some twenty-five miles further on, lies the town of Gytheion with full facilities. It is little visited by yachts and could be uncomfortable, even untenable, with the wind in its present direction, so we make up our minds to try our luck in Porto Kaio. Next we encounter the seam in the Gulf waters where opposing seas meet and take a dislike to one another. With white water chopping at the hull, anything seems better than being churned about in a maelstrom, so when the wind suddenly backs south, by then the light fading, we alter course north to 334 degrees for Gytheion, the Captain conserving battery power by restricting its use to the light above the chart table. With a further wind increase in our favour, we hoist the full main and genoa, and I keep lookout to allow my Pets to study the Admiralty chart by torchlight.

What we need is a coastline profile (preferably by Admiralty artist, Commander Graves) but none is available. Distance flattens forms. Headlands and bays merge into a canvas-thin backdrop. However, in the opinion of Zanthoula and myself, the darker landmasses had to be obtruding capes. By this means we identify Cape Kolokithia ("Cape Vegetable Marrow") and, further north, Scoutari, after which the land fades, falling back. We judge a particularly dark projection beyond to be Mavrovouni (Black Mountain). Then, from behind Mavrovouni, a tall, octagonal lighthouse materialises – and we know we have made Gytheion.

After twenty-seven hours and 121.85 nautical miles, at an average speed of 4.6 kts, our lines are taken on Gytheion waterfront. "Hey there, Pussy Cat! Come and fish!" the children call. I leap ashore at once. The prize I take home is a gecko, which I lose. Zanthoula discovers it three days later covered in carpet fluff and minus its tail, but otherwise fit for release. I never do encounter any of the plump brown quails beloved of the Maniots. (This is perhaps fortunate for the quails.)

Boat-shaped Kranai Island is linked by a causeway to Gytheion quay. Providing a grandstand for the voluptuous sunsets of the High Taigetos, it is where the runaways Helen of Troy and Paris spent their first night of love. It also turns out to be a setting for a rom com of my own, for I spend several nights in passionate pursuit of "Lady", who lives on a German yacht. Then Lady's Pet calls round to tell my Pets, with obvious amusement, that not only am I keeping them awake at night, but that this particular Lady Helen is old enough to be my grandmother (in fact several times over) and does not feel up to the attentions of a young buck like me. Well! It's her loss!

After a boat trip exploring the subterranean Caves of Douro, we leave for the Deep Mani, a finger of land dominated by grim villages of Dark Age peel towers resembling giant mushroom stalks. At the end of the peninsula I guide us into Porto Kaio. No pirates are at home, but dark waves splash my Pets' faces as they swim to make sure the anchor is bedded. Later, winds heavy with ghostly voices gust over the saddle and a nightmarish atmosphere disturbs our sleep. So apprehensive am I, I do not stay on deck, but go down into the cabin to curl up in the crook of Zanthoula's knees.

Porto Kaio, the slave trade its mainspring, abounds in ghosts. We have heard them moaning. The abandoned monastery, where traces of human remains have been discovered, was once the site of a Temple of Poseidon.

Next day, we up anchor at crack of dawn, without pausing for early tea. Outside the atmosphere lightens, and so do our spirits.

EIGHTEEN

I Salute an Icon and Exit Greek Waters

In which I salute scholar-gipsy Patrick Leigh Fermor.

From Kalamata we sail for Katakolon, Zakynthos and Kefalonia.

Exiting Greek waters, I join the diaspora.

Five steps from the shoreline in nearby Asomato Bay lies the ancient Gate of Hell, a grotto later adopted as a store by smugglers and fishermen. I am thankful there is no storm to rouse the Hell Hound Cerebus from his slumbers within.

The Mani crouches like a grey wolf, nose on paws, haunches raised, to end at Cape Tainaron where the Taigetos mountains peter out. When we pass by the lighthouse to enter the Messenian Gulf the swell tumbles us horribly. Roller-coasting through a slovenly sea we struggle to pass the endless toad-slimy bastion of Capo Grosso, unable to sail faster, though it is no place to linger:

> Stay forty miles
> Off Cape Tainaron
> And twice forty more again
> Off Capo Grosso

Exuding its own brand of chthonic power, Capo Grosso seems to go on forever. Once we are within the shelter of the outer arm of the Messenian Gulf, however, the sea smooths and we glide past Kardamili, home to scholar-gipsy Patrick Leigh Fermor. I would have liked to make his acquaintance, for not only do we share a favourite book in *Winnie ille Pu* but, more importantly, I know his heart is in the right place. for he and his wife, Joan, are devoted to Greek cats. They say the feral population, to which they opened their doors, stabilised at around twenty to twenty-five felines. All are made welcome and fed and may come and go as they please.

As we pass Kardamili, a day sailer packed with small children puts out to circle us. Zanthoula lifts me up to wave and the children cheer and blow kisses. My wave is for Mr Leigh Fermor too.

The town of Kalamata, its harbour entrance anything but obvious from out at sea through a thick mist, is one of those places described as "easily identifiable" in the pilot. However, for a Ship's Cat with a sharp nose for landfall, identification, as we close the coast, is not too trying, and we ease our way in. Time for a sundowner. An old man on the quay tries to tempt me with a toffee, which, needless to say, is not to my taste. He ends by dropping a whole packet of sweeties on deck as a conversation starter. He is a bit of a dafty, it must be admitted. Spotting him springing up and down like Zebedee one day and, hearing his shout of "Καπετάνιο! Καπετάνιο! Βαρκάκι! ΓΡΗΓΟΡΑ!" ("Captain! Captain! Dinghy! QUICKLY!") I alert the Captain to an emergency. It appears that Grandad (possibly after a glass or two) had attempted both to untie his fishing-smack and hang on to it while boarding. Having failed abysmally on both counts, he has been forced to witness his sizeable craft drifting out of harbour unmanned. The Captain loses no time in bundling the old salt into our dinghy and rowing for dear life. Catching up with his renegade boat and shoving Grandad aboard, he leaves him to it, still cackling merrily.

The perpendicular heights of Mount Taigetos rear up beside us. These empty crags are the home of Artemis in her guise as Keeper of the Wild

Things. When the mad-dog sun plagues us, having visions of Makrynas, the Faraway One, the Great God Pan, I crawl into the dank shade of the harbour wall remembering that Pan's was the ghost that stalked in the mid-day sun.

On the far side of the Messian Gulf the hills are boringly low and the scenery distressingly bland. How I miss the astringency of the Aegean world as we home in on the pepper-pot Tower of Bourdzi with its willow-pattern bridge. "Cheer up, Wackster!" say my Pets, pulling my ears, which usually does the trick. Navarino Bay beyond is famous as the site of the last major battle between sailing ships. It does make me feel better when we pass its entrance to think of all the Ships' Cats who must have played their part in battle. Would I have measured up? You bet I would.

At down-at-heel Katakolon on the peninsula beyond, described as "shaped like a cross-section of an aeroplane" and which we nearly miss, the acrid smell of wildfire invades our nostrils. Heavy-bellied Canadair planes circle the bay, swooping to water-bomb the encroaching forest fires.

Despite serving as a Port of Entry, Katakolon lacks both a fuel station and a bank. Once it serviced the currant trade. Now it services cruise liners. We join the smaller craft on an apron quay fronting waste ground. Evening brings the pumped-out renderings of the songs of the moment "Σαγαπώ" ("I love you") and "Καλό καλοκαίρι" ("Have a good summer).

When my Pets go off to Olympia, I take the opportunity to inspect the yacht next door on account of its interesting smell. This is explained, I discover, by it being a sort of floating doggery-cum-cattery for four dogs and four cats, all uncertificated and undeclared. They tell me their Dutch owner does not hold with regulations. What a sad life they live. Not one of them is ever allowed ashore.

As soon as a Lederhosen Band sponsored by the Austrian State Tourist Board parades, a Ferris wheel is erected beside *Cappelle* and a light aircraft flies overhead advertising the imminence of a Bier Fest, we press on.

I am eager to see both Kefalonia, the island which provided the spruce for Odysseus's masts, and Zakynthos, whose tar pools were used in their preservation. As we draw into Zakynthos we were delighted to see yachtsmen filling their water canisters from a quayside standpipe. The pulverising heat persuades me to flop into the darkest corner of the cabin, blue curtains drawn, while Zanthoula dashes off down the white sand beach to fall into the sea with a splash, an act she repeats every morning. (In fact I suspect that some mornings she wakes up in it!) She makes a friend called Antigone and they paddle around together exchanging girl-talk.

When we leave Zakynthos for the north we pass its famous Blue Caves all aglow with turquoise reflections. Then, as soon as Cape Skinari bears 270 degrees, we force *Cappelle* out through uneven furrows of water into the channel that divides Zakynthos from Kefalonia. Here edge-dancing shearwaters squabble over fish. It is hard going. By midday the nor' nor' westerly, described in the Pilot as "hair-raising", is living up to its name. I keep watch as we give Kekova Shallows a wide berth, only for the wind to force us further and further into Kefalonia's eight-mile steep-to lee of Mount Aetos (Mount Eagle), a brooding mountain. Its awareness of us makes the fur on the back of my neck stand up.

Our aim is to make passage into the Gulf of Argostoli, fouled as it is on both sides by underwater rocks and reefs. However, both the strong winds and Mount Aetos have other ideas, driving us towards a mighty molar, known as Thionisi, on which once stood a Temple of Zeus. Meanwhile winds as hard as willow bats zap us on the nose. "Poor vision in filthy head sea!" writes the Captain in the log. I agree, though I can see better than he can, until Zanthoula, fearing for my safety, is officious enough to shut me below.

By 18.00 hrs my Pets have to acknowledge that Thionisi now lies slightly aft. To starboard instead rears the Aspra Vraska ("The White Rocks") of St Nicholas Point. Here the saint once reigned in his aspect of Blue-bearded Poseidon. Since we were now over the edge of the very shoal we have been trying so hard to avoid, I pray he is not in a malevolent mood. At 19.15 hrs our destination of Argostoli hoves in sight two miles down the inlet behind a wooded spit. This means we must pay strict attention to buoyage and to the fishing nets laid around us.

None of us has eaten all day and much of the stowage is on the floor. Zanthoula throws her usual fit when she can't find me. I know where I am all right. I am in the safest spot I can think of, the cubbyhole above the wet wardrobe. Gasping with relief when she sees me crouching there, she feeds me tidbits while attempting to tidy up. When we look back across the blue-black waters in the light of evening, Zakynthos, an island that has taken us all day to escape, looks close enough to touch.

We moor on Argostoli's Customs Quay among quarantine-flagged arrivals from Italy. Ten metres off quay, an Essex couple on Moody *Wild Mood* wave bottles of gin while holding up their Ship's Cat, "Pudding". What a pudding, she is, too. They dumped their anchor off quay, they say, being too exhausted to manoeuvre nearer after sailing from Italy. With only one mooring ring free, someone fixes our second warp to the hawser of a ferry they insist is laid up. I dance ashore hoping to engage Pudding in a Pudding chase. She isn't keen.

Cats are top of the pops in the Ionian this year, the song Η γατούλα μου μικρή ("My Little Pussycat") blares out on all sides. I like Argostoli. (Pudding likes it less. She is uncomfortable with my chasing games, but they do get her blood moving.) A Greek lady on a VIP yacht takes a shine to me and comes to tell my Pets she has witnessed my nightly jaunts up the ferry's gangplank. These are unwise, she says. You never know with ferries. She is glad to see the Evil Eye on my collar, a tried and true protection since ancient times, she says, telling us of a Greek vessel dating to the fourth century BC found with Evil Eyes painted each side of its prow. If my amulet should ever be mislaid it should be replaced forthwith, for "Αυτό είναι πάμα πολύ σγμαντικί!" ("It is most important!") Even though this lady so admires me, I refuse to let her pick me up. This enchants her. "It is you he loves!" she coos to Zanthoula.

There are jobs for the Captain to complete, red tape to comply with and forms to apply for prior to leaving for Italy. There is also the dinghy to scrape, scrub and pack, not to mention our torn genoa to replace with its reconstituted original, no easy task for us in stultifying heat with a heavy swell running. The sun gets in our eyes as the halyards twist in light airs. Obliterated in flapping canvas, Zanthoula and I are nearly knocked overboard twice. Even then the Captain insists on raising sail several times to make sure the set is right.

When all is shipshape, Zanthoula takes a local bus to the other side of the island in order to look down on Ithaca, Odysseus's homeland, for without Odysseus our journey might never have started. It is sad to bid goodbye to friends new and old, one of whom remembers me as the "little rabbit" who, long ago in the days of his youth, shot down the porthole in Mitilini.

On our last night on the converted Sottish trawler beside, Captain Stamati sings to himself as he cradles his mandolin. The syncopated recitative etches itself into our heads like an echo of Greece.

The next day we turn out into the Ionian Sea and set our course due west. After we clear the light on Cape Yerogamba the wind frees, while from the north we hear the last echo of the death cry of the Great God Pan when vanquished by a new religion Then *Cappelle* settles down to ride the dependable blow. We take two-hour watches, myself with Zanthoula. As I gaze at the stars, I am aware that, part of my people's diaspora, I am sailing away from the land of my birth for ever. "Isambard Kingdom Brunel!" I murmur to myself. I don't know what it means. I think it's a name. But it is suitably sonorous for a mantra and is another phrase I repeat when I feel need to calm the nerves.

NINETEEN

Landfall in Italy

In which I mistake a ship for a lighthouse.
I become the first crew member to step on Italian soil.

At 07.15 hrs on the third morning, the sun breasts the band of mist on the horizon. Hold it. No land in sight. At 9 o'clock I let out a "Land Ahoy!" cry loud enough to initiate an energy rush that launches my Pets into a madcap tidy-up. What I have seen, so I believed, is the lighthouse on Cape Spartivento, landmark for the toe of Italy. But there is a problem. On returning on deck in clean shirts ready to meet officialdom, my Pets are disconcerted to find my landmark shifted to port. I am deeply discomforted, of course, but compromise by saying "Isambard Kingdom Brunel" three times and going off duty for a short sharp sulk to regain composure. My mistake, it is now evident, has been to confuse a lighthouse with that moveable feast – the superstructure of a supertanker steaming out of the Straits of Messina between Italy and Sicily.

The next shock occurs when the emergent coastline disappears. We must be off course! Back on again, after a massive compass swing has righted itself, it is only after another hour and 20 minutes that the Captain positively identifies Cape Spartivento backed by the lion-coloured hills of Calabria. (Compass swings should not come as a surprise in a historic battle area in which the sea bed is encumbered with wartime debris.)

Once we have coped with the violent oops-a-daisy of the tide race issuing out of the Straits, we hoist the Italian courtesy flag. After that it is a question of me holding my nerve while Zanthoula and the Captain climb onto the coachroof to hand the sails before *Cappelle* lurches through Salina Joniche's narrow entrance. This man-made white elephant of a haven, part of a so-called factory development built, in all probability, to line the pockets of the Mafia, had lately been assigned to the convenience of small boats before and after passage of the Straits. There is the usual argy-bargy when Zanthoula fails to hold the boathook straight while attempting to grab a rung of the iron ladder on the far wall. When she succeeds, we find ourselves in a vast and isolated concrete tank of unruffled blue water, perfect shelter for exhausted yachtsmen and Ship's Cats. (Indeed, Salina Joniche is almost too secure, for its high sides blank off radio signals, making it impossible to obtain weather forecasts.)

On mounting the wall ladder, the Captain reports the wasteland above a suitable playground for a Ship's Cat. He then proceeds to coach me in climbing onto the boom to undertake a vertical leap onto the top of the quay wall, a difficult task, which requires a double kick-off. My attitude in situations like this is to think my way through the problem ahead, and then do my best to act out my think. This usually works.

Once up there, all I am able to see of my ship is the tip of her mast. After a cursory exploration of the weed-strewn ground with its abandoned narrow-gauge rail track, I realise how peckish I am and go down again to see what has spawned in my blue bowl. (It is good to keep an eye on it.) It is easy to judge my return jump onto the boom, but it does make *Cappelle* rock. Bump! The boom shakes as I land, then comes a secondary bump, lighter this time, as I hop on deck. I carry this feat out twice nightly, without mishap, all the time we remain in spooky Salina Joniche.

Though we have officially exited Greek waters, I still look around with Greek-orientated eyes, happy to learn that we are now in Magna Graecia. Since the southern Italians here are said to share more DNA with the Greeks than with their northern Italian compatriots, basically, I hadn't left home at all. I also feel the old tickle of ancestral recognition when I remember that this stretch of coast saw the first importation into Europe of *cattus domesticus* employed in Egypt to protect the grain stores from rats.

First off I plan to seek out the church of St George dedicated to the Madonna della Gattiola, the Virgin of the Cat Flap. In the fifteenth century, when the church was built, the Madonna's likeness was painted on a door panel. However, when the church was plagued by mice at a later date the new priest ordered a cat flap to be cut right through the Our Lady's portrait, believing it important to allow the church cat freedom of access. Our Lady thus became known as the Virgin of the Cat Flap.

Next morning a customs boat on routine circuit enters Salina Joniche. Casually it salutes our Italian flag without requesting sight of our *Constituto in arrivo per il naviglio da disporto* (permit to sail Italian waters), which details our crew and particulars. After the Captain has checked the batteries and effected minor boat repairs, we can no longer put off consideration of the tidal flow in the Straits, our next challenge. This is far from easy to estimate. All my Pets have to assist us are the phases of the moon in Zanthoula's pocket diary – on the basis that tides are weakest when the moon is out of line with the sun (full moon and dark of moon being the periods of strong tides to avoid.)

At this point *Musu*, a pretty gaff-rigged replica of a Falmouth oyster boat, travelling south, with a Dutch couple on board, plus a big soppy dog of Dutch breed too old to leave behind in Holland, joins us. Bölle, the dog, turns out to be a right wimp, crying non-stop over nothing – that's dogs for you! My Pets ask the couple how best to tackle the Straits, but they

have little to say about the passage, except that they were obliged to abort their first attempt. Since Tide Tables for the Straits of Gibraltar relevant to the Straits of Messina (with the application of the necessary adjustments) are impossible to obtain, the only advice they could get was "not to go if the ferries have stopped!" In any case, as the Straits are twenty-five miles long, a change of tide is inevitable. We would necessarily experience both the *montante* or north-flowing current and the *scendente* or south-flowing stream.

TWENTY

Wacky and Odysseus

In which we brave Scylla and Charybdis.
I suffer a funny turn that reveals a past life.
We survive a fireworks display.

At 06.05 hours next morning we hoist sail within our concrete womb before emerging under engine into an amphitheatre of swordfish boats. These are rowed with sweeps, the skipper directing his craft for the harpooner in the bows from a chair at the top of the short mast. The swordfish fleet is a welcome sight, since its presence indicates calm conditions.

On the Sicilian side of the Straits opposite us as we emerge, rears the clumsy bulk of Mongibello (a local name for Mount Etna). Villagers consider her their mother, who feeds and protects those who live on her slopes. She has seldom maimed or killed – but when she has erupted, it has sometimes been devastating! If she stirs enough to prompt flight, it is customary for the villagers to leave food and wine on the table to placate the tired and angry God of Fire.

I look back to see a peachy horizon backlighting the bubbling black rock formations of Calabria. At Punta Pellaro, hemmed in by rugged brown hills, we turn dead centre into the Straits. As we do so, I experience one of my funny turns. "Get a grip," I tell myself. It is essential to keep a firm hold on reality. But this swimmy feeling has nothing to do with sailing – a gybe or a near miss. Neither is it connected with the state of the sea. It is just something that plays havoc with my equilibrium, as if my world and its space-time turn topsy-turvy without warning, jerking at the memory cells and causing me – but not quite – to remember something. But what?

"Watch it, Wackster. Pay attention." On each side of us a yacht hugs the shore, while another ahead dices chirpily with the shipping. ("Got to be a Frenchman," mutters the Captain.) With a *montante* bearing us swiftly onwards and clouds of white butterflies fluttering round our heads, we make steady progress, though we must keep our eyes open to spot the die-hard wind-surfers off the beaches of Reggio di Calabria intent on playing last across the bows. (I give the Captain a quick nip, if I think he isn't aware of an approach.) Four miles ahead, Mississippi-style ferries with powerful turbines, plying relentlessly from Reggio di Calabria to Messina and back, are strung out across the straits, scarce hesitating before embarking on the return trip. Then, despite added engine revolutions, our speed drops, indicating the tide has turned and we are headed by a *scendente,* though of no great strength. The six ferries, three from each side, that criss-cross our path bring to our attention the fact that we have failed to compute the Ferragosto, the Italian manual workers' holiday in August into our problem factors.

Meanwhile we try to work out whether to direct our increasingly sluggish progress across ferry bows or wait to cross sterns. Either way we must enter the churning conveyor belts of opposing shipping. Then comes the second line of ferries travelling obliquely from Villa San Geovanni on the mainland to Messina on Sicily. I try not to shut my eyes as the ferries, three from each side, bear down on us as inexorably as streams of lava. But we continue without incident. At midday, Zanthoula takes a bearing of 90 deg E on the giant red-and-white striped barber's pole of Punta Pezzo light structure and we contemplate the narrows angled ahead.

I began to feel light-headed again and think I see a fairy castle build up in the air. (As long ago as the sixth century BC, the Fata Morgana, a sort of superior mirage believed created by witchcraft, was reported in the area.) I am finding it hard to know what is real and what is not. Now we are confronted by hideous gate posts like something intergalactic. These weighty pylons supporting heavy coils of electricity cable carry power from the mainland across to Sicily. Shipping is warned they show on radar and that all Straits traffic must pass beneath.

To port the waters seethe like a fish feeding ground or the frantic rotation of rapids over pebbles. "Welcome to Charybdis," says the Captain. My heart misses a beat. The earthquake of 1824 has calmed the sea bed and the weather is good, so conditions are favourable, but I still hear the name "Charybdis" with a shudder. Then, before I can draw breath, there is a *bouleversement* in my head and a portal opens onto another world, giving a glimpse of another time, another space. Teetering on shaky paws, I pull back from the brink.

What I glimpse through the gap in time is Odysseus's Ship-of-No-Name, a handsome trireme manned by twelve oarsmen in three rows. Without a doubt, I know I had once worked as Ship's Cat on that trireme as it made passage through the Straits. On account of my previous experience, Artemis has now despatched me on another such mission, this time as guardian of a modern odyssey, a small one may be and a good sight more technical, but you might call it "copycat".

On Odysseus's ship my job specification was primarily one of rodent officer. Of course, I did not presume to offer Odysseus professional advice but, while carrying out his commands, trained myself to be a full member of crew. My most valuable asset was my phenomenal night-sight. Positioning myself beside my master on night passages I heeded timely whispers in my ear from my muse astronomer, Urania, as I assisted with astro-navigation. (Middle-aged Odysseus was a romantic, let's face it, "never closing his eyes but keeping them on the Pleiades". I ask you.) My sense of smell was useful too. Aware of my ability to sniff land from a distance, Bisto-kid style, I raised the antennae of my whiskers to pick up scent; a flower-filled zephyr from an island, the sweet stink of rotting flesh from a battlefield, the aroma of herbs drying on a rack, the hunger-aching smells arising from cooking pots or the odour of a sacrificial roast, all alerted me as to our position.

Knowing how homesick our crew were, I took upon myself the job of oarsmen minder and furry comforter. The rowers, dreaming of their homeland, lead a tough life, as indeed we all did. As Nikos Gatsos said of Amorgos,

> "Their own country is tied in their sails
> And oars hang in the wind."

To starboard, just as it had in the days of the Ship-of-No-Name, rears a volcanic plug shaped like a squared-off tree trunk. On the pool in front is scarcely a ripple. Here Scylla, daughter of Hecate, lies dormant, though Circe warned Odysseus, "Scylla was not born for Death, that fiend will live for ever!" (I would not trust her either in a November squall.)

Back in the present once more I hear Zanthoula telling the Captain she has been keeping her eye on the log reading and that we just notched up 1,000 nautical miles for the current sailing season.

As we exit the Straits the image of the trireme fades. To starboard instead appears the volcanic plug I saw in my vision. But it has changed, for now it is surmounted by a fortress. The village of Scylla, described in the Pilot as "quiet, safe and peaceful", lies in wings each side. Taken aback by what lies behind the mole, for the harbour bears no relation to its plan in the Pilot, we give it a good offing to avoid reported underwater debris from storm damage. A new mole at right angles – presently encumbered by a cement mixer and an assortment of building plant – is under construction, while dodgy left-over sections of the old wall are taped off. Moreover what space remains is chock-a-block with every type of ill-assorted, ill-parked craft imaginable. When we swing away for urgent discussion, my Pets spot a note in the Pilot warning that Scylla is "only safe in calm conditions" – so we might be required to escape in a hurry. At that moment the lone sailing yacht inside chooses to leave and we move in to take her place, beneath us a crosshatch of anchor chains and slimy rocks. Despite agitation on my part, the Captain does not pause to prepare the anchor or knot an extra warp onto the chain.

If we are asking for trouble, we get it, jerking up short of the quay. Then, when we do move forward, it is to find the quay devoid of mooring rings and the bollards out of reach. This leads to what I can only describe as an altercation between my Pets. (Not pretty, you may say!) It becomes essential to shackle on a riding weight. At one point the weight sinks the Captain instead of the other way round. Then in clambering back on board retching his heart out, he knocks our best boat hook overboard. (Draw a veil! Let them sort it out!) According to the Captain it is something to do with Zanthoula never having learnt to throw a line properly. She begs to differ.

It may sound mean, but I see fit to make myself scarce. After all I am anxious to come to terms with the locals, not just the trampling hordes of human beans but the feline crowd too. It has not taken me long to notice the place is full of cats: young 'uns, old 'uns, skinny 'uns, not many fat 'uns, scabby 'uns, street fighters, caterwaulers, slinkers, thugs, thieves, stripeys, mangey types and waifs. I am on the path of Norman Douglas's cats of Old Calabria, "haggard, shifty and careworn, their ears atremble".

When next I see Zanthoula she is off for a walk with her nose in the air, wearing her best pink kanga. (Swish! Swish!) After the Captain has secured his ship like Fort Knox, my Pets meet up again oh-so-casually and set off together along the roofed road that runs round the base of the rock; I follow at a discrete distance. (I see they are holding hands.) The air smells enticingly of shellfish, mozzarella, herbs and pasta. (The diet in this part of Italy is reputed to be the best in the world. But will we ever get a taste of it?) We pass the grotto of the evil witch Scylla, which makes me thankful to be in company, for here the wicked nymph had been wont to snore, replete with sailors, fish, and ships' cats. Now her grotto is sanctified by a statue of a *gentilissa* Madonna, a hedge of candles set before her to celebrate her Assumption.

When Zanthoula slips into the Straits for a swim, all she can see on the sea bed are water-magnified Coca Cola tins. I think she expected the whitened bones of sailors and ships' cats, or perhaps the pearls that were the eyes of Parthenope, who drowned herself after failing to seduce Odysseus. Seaweed was her bridal wreath, shells were her dowry. I was there when Odysseus lashed himself to the mast and plugged the ears of his crew to prevent them being won over by the sweet songs of the Sirens. But all this is in another life.

We do not get back to *Cappelle* until it is growing dark. The Captain just has time to unlock the cabin doors before the fortress blows its top in a sky-high explosion – or so it seems – and a panic-struck, *"sauve qui peut"* Ship's Cat (me) forces itself between his legs to flee inside and dive behind the spare water tank. At the same time the Captain and Zanthoula both duck instinctively, almost scared enough to follow me. It is but the overture to a bombardment that heralds a grand fireworks display. Rockets swoosh, Catherine wheels whizz, firecrackers explode, Roman candles perform whining parabolas and multi-coloured rain fountains across the skies. All is punctuated every few seconds by more 1812-style cannonades. Our eyes never have time to recover from the retinal impact of one explosion before the next sears the eyeballs, not a moment wasted and all too close for comfort. Burnt-out debris patters in the water around us. I know it then – **THE ITALIAN NATION IS OUT TO GET ME!** We think we must have put in to Scylla on Carnival Night. But it transpires that every night is Carnival Night during the Ferragosto, the two-week holiday period. (But, whatever anyone says, it is ME they are after, I am certain. I have no wish to linger longer in Scylla.)

Despite the enticing smell, my Pets suffer hunger pangs, and so do I. For me to grab a fresh bite means competing with the manky locals and probably a punch-up. It is different for my Pets. Their problem is that they had no Italian lire. Obtaining cash is not easy. We are now in one of the most crime-infested areas of Southern Italy where life is cheap and piracy rife. But it is my Pets who are under suspicion. Shuffling its feet, the queue at the bank stare at them. When asked to give their address, the name of a boat means nothing. Finally, having signed enough forms to fill a filing cabinet, being photographed and having their passports photocopied, they are awaiting finger-printing when a bank official relents and permits them to take out enough lire to feed themselves.

They leave feeling like Bonnie and Clyde. Once outside, Zanthoula, polishing her best Italian – she has learnt only one phrase, "*Supermercato, per favore!*" – accosts a young Lothario in swimming trunks with a towel round his neck. Immediately he beckon my Pets round a corner. What they expect to see is a store, but what they find is a tiny Fiat car into which he squeezes them both before setting off at breakneck speed to the top of the Rock where he drops them outside a big supermarket, before, waving a cheery goodbye, he careers away again down to his delayed swim. Thus they are able to spend their money at local prices on a wide variety of delicious fruit, fresh vegetables, pasta, pesto, prosciutto, parmesan, shell fish, fish for cats, you name it, ciabatta, chianti and tiramisu.

Their steps are light as they skip back to *Cappelle* down stepped alleyways, and through courtyards dangling with strings of washing and ablaze with flower-filled petrol cans, where men in grubby vests sit scratching their bellies. Far below they can see the *bastardi,* whose eddies and counter-eddies frame the satin-smooth waters of what had once been Scylla's lair. It is downhill all the way.

TWENTY-ONE

Mugged in the Aeolians

In which we explore a volcanic archipelago.
Cappelle is boarded by The Little Mafiosi
I am mugged and my Pets take a hot mud bath.

We do not dally in Scylla, I am thankful to say, because of fuel shortage and because the harbour tap offers only rust and beetles. Assisting a German yacht, we raise anchors and both move out, the Germans to winter in Malta, *Cappelle* to sail thirty-five miles northwest to the Aeolian islands. Here we hope to fare better. Here too the Warden of the Winds gave Odysseus a bag containing, not the desired treasure, but contrary winds. I promise myself to fill in my diary, if conditions allow.

An island takes shape ahead. This is Vulcano. The Aeolians are known as "The Floating Isles" from their seeming ability to manifest themselves by drifting in and out of sight out of mist. Catching a glimpse of a parrot-green valley ahead, we follow boats approaching Porto di Levante where yachts and ferries jostle for position. On the chaotic waterfront a milling, south-sea-island-style mob presses flesh to flesh.

My Pets have been informed that an official Ormeggiatori is in charge of Aeolian quays to help yachtsmen tie up, keep an eye on their boat and supply water. We have also been warned by Leo in Tinos, who suffered a bad experience in Volcano, on no account to fall into the clutches of the Little Mafiosi, piratical youngsters who hold yachtsmen to ransom. We are to discover avoidance of them is easier said than done.

When another yacht backs off the quay we move forward. As we do so, an innocent-looking teenager larking about in the water, grabs one of our warps and expertly tosses it to a girl in a bikini sitting on the quay idly swinging her legs. Our warp is yanked tightly round a bollard as three more youths haul themselves over the bows. The first move of the leader is to grab me by the scruff and dangle me over the side on the pretence of apprehending a stray animal the Captain will want throwing in. I claw out in vain, petrified and too choked to breathe or turn my head to bite. It is a moment of blind terror. This is distraction enough for Zanthoula as she fights to rescue me. Meanwhile another young mafioso pushes past to dive into the cabin, the Captain after him, the youth protesting he is looking for a bucket to wash the deck (more like to steal what he can (as, in Leo's case, his binoculars). The whole charade is played out in a briskly dominating style of tomfoolery, as if we are under invasion by a swarm of monkeys.

Our situation is saved when a glossier fish, a larger and more expensive yacht, draws in alongside. At this I am unceremoniously let fall on deck as all three lads leap-frog over our side rails onto the yacht next door. "They'll be back!" says the Captain grimly. He then has words with an Italian skipper, who tells him the gang will return to demand money and that it is safer to pay up rather than risk retaliation. On no account give too much, he advises. Sure enough, they swagger back, the leader demanding money with menaces. He balls his fists at the sum offered, but his companion snatches the money and they run off.

Later Zanthoula spots the gang ashore drawing on what looked like reefers while doing deals with a pair of North Africans. Traumatised, I stay below. The Captain describes Porto di Levante in the log as "frantic and impossible". We fear the mafiosi may return that night until, to our relief, it becomes evident they left for Palermo on the last ferry of the day.

Beyond the rubbish-strewn street I glimpse the weird beauties of nature, tufa-eroded shapes in psychedelic colours, sulphuric yellow, burnt orange, heliotrope and Tyrrhenian pink, all aglow in the late afternoon sun. Zanthoula insists on exploring. Off she goes wearing a floaty pareo tied hipster-style over her bikini, a style she copied from the bimboes on the luxury yacht next door. Neither can she resist a hot mud wallow. I stay home. My Pets come back exuding the appalling smell of bad eggs. God forbid. I can't sleep that night, whining in my half-sleep and sneezing violently to rid myself of the foul expirations. Post-traumatic stress. That's what. In the morning the Captain declares, "The Ship's Cat does not wish to stay here and neither do I." He never spoke a truer word.

Port Lipari, on the adjoining island of the name, is almost deserted at midday. Here we receive a friendly welcome from an official Ormeggiatori, an elderly Popeye in white ducks and yachting cap. Tying *Cappelle's* mooring rope to a pavement grating, he straightens her up and ties her other rope to another pavement grating further along the quay. Then, saying, "British good!" Very nice!" and "British soldier call me 'Jack'," he leaves with a salute, promising to provide water, which is delivered to these waterless Aeolians by naval tanker.

That night I dream of fleecy, snub-nosed old goat-man Papposilenos Simos who, in classic times, was tightly bound with thongs of flowers and, when fighting drunk, left to sleep it off in a rose garden, while the white doves of Aphrodite circle about his head and laugh at him. But Papposilenos didn't have the Little Mafiosi to contend with like we did!

Popeye Jack is our champion. He even boxes the ears of a budding Mini Mussolini all of seven years old, who swings on *Cappelle's* warps before turning round to wiggle his bottom at Zanthoula as she tries to board, spitting at her feet and calling her "Americana", until other children shout she is "Inglese" and all right. That night I let Jack pick me up when we say goodbye. We give him a big bowl for his fish, as well as a tip, while he assures us a welcome will always await us in Lipari.

As we pull away from the Aeolian Islands, Gran Cratere, every schoolboy's dream volcano, is in action, spewing forth soot-black smoke They say that molten magma continues to build in the Aeolians. One villager had assured us there will always be sufficient time to evacuate an island before an eruption, adding, "Except perhaps in August." I look around half-expecting to see the Brothers Barbarossa, the gentian waters alive with black ships full of gewgaws, death-dealing corsairs and Ship's Cats with cutlasses in their teeth.

We arrange our time of departure, not only to clear the islands before surface nets are laid, but to sail within the orbit of Stromboli, the "Lighthouse of the Mediterranean" to witness what Zanthoula splendidly refers to as the "geo-poetry of its fire-fountain", which has captured her imagination. Circe, in another life, gave Odysseus a warning about this fiery salvo when she invited him to dine, telling him not to approach too close or he might end up as flotsam licked by Stromboli's tempestuous flames. I think of my Greek countrymen, the Knidians, whom Aphrodite Euploia had guided all the way from Knidos to the Aeolian Islands, 2,500 years ago, just as she guided *Cappelle* in the present day.

By the time we reach the northern end of the island of Salina, dusk is settling at sea level, while, in the upper air, its dying rays pin-point the frail houses on the rim of Salina's awful steep-to crater wall. Menaced in shadow, we sail beneath as the wall it stares down at us. As the evening chill comes on, the fearsomeness of nature is a reminder of what a fragile-winged moth we are, with hardly more control of our destiny than a blown leaf, about to leave the questionable shelter of a volcanic archipelago at night for the open perils of a ring of fire. Here the sea emits a sulphurous whiff, while the floating dandruff of pumice dust demonstrates the area's instability. Pumice dust is a reminder that only five hundred metres beneath us

sleeps the super-volcano Marsili, as high as Mount Etna beneath the waves.

Despite the land's disinterest, there remains an urge to cling to it, but we sail on towards the last cape of Salina and a rock arch framing the void "wherethrough / gleams that untravelled world / whose margin fades for ever and for ever when I move" – as Tennyson's Ulysses/Odysseus puts it. Except for the dimly seen cone of Filicudi to the west and Stromboli to the east, only empty water lies ahead. By 20.00 hrs darkness has engulfed the islands.

TWENTY-TWO

Stromboli

In which we witness a Fire Fountain.
A four-legged stowaway makes his presence felt.
Crossing the Bouches de Bonifacio, we sail on for Corsica.

O h God!" Just look!" exclaims Zanthoula. At that moment in the distance ahead the giant lava lamp that is Stromboli bursts apart, shooting its spectacular fire fountain into the night sky as it has done at ten-minute intervals from time immemorial, the perfect navigational direction indicator. Bearing west, as we move under engine across windless waters I seek the company of Zanthoula and the Captain, who is engaged in strapping the radio to the coach roof to listen to a running commentary from the BBC World Service (something world-changing about a Mr Gorbachev's disappearance.)

At 22.00 hrs we settle to two-hour watches. Above us the Pleiades form a crystal parachute. (Don't ask for the moon. We are the lucky ones who have the shooting stars.) Slowly night elides with day to illumine a windless, olive oil sea. The sails slat lazily. It is far too hot. All next day, the seconds stretch out like rubber bands, the microwaved air vibrates heat. We are a minimum of a hundred miles from land in any direction, there is no wind and the generator has ceased to function. The Captain spends the next night tracing a fault.

Perched on the hatch, I concentrate on my toilet. "When in doubt, wash!" is a tip I picked up from Jennie Baudrons, Paul Gallico's cat. It is a wise maxim. I am not exactly in doubt, but concentrating on grooming helps relaxation. I become aware of something. Paw raised, I listen, There it is again, the mystery sound! I squeeze my eyes in Zanthoula's direction, but she fails to catch on. Only later, when she discovers teeth marks in a chocolate wrapper, are my suspicions confirmed. We have picked up a stowaway. Of course, it is my bounden duty, as Ship's Cat, to apprehend the interloper, but I am in a particularly laid-back mood. It does rouse me when Zanthoula discovers a hole in the carton of cat biscuits stored under the floorboards, but not enough to encourage me to make an effort. I am clearly not of the same persuasion as Robinson Crusoe's cats, who shielded their master from mice. Indeed our stowaway would not be easy to catch, since intelligent use of the spacing between the boat frames enables it to remain free range, having instant access to, as well as escape from, all lockers via the back door, so to speak.

For over 110 miles in a straight line from Cape Cabonara to Cape Coda Cavallo, the hostile coast of Sardinia has remained unchanged since the days of Pausanias, who described it as "an unbroken chain of impassable mountains without anchorage". We are now aiming not for the Costa Smeralda, the most expensive location in Europe, but for Olbia, described as a reasonable town with good workshops albeit "rather dirty", to seek repairs to the generator.

The trouble with me is that when I get bored, I get peevish. Zanthoula knows the signs and does her best to distract me. Accordingly, she engages me in a rumble-tumble in the cabin. This consists of Zanthoula throwing cushions and me dodging and tunnelling under duvets to pop out somewhere unexpected. It is a good game, though it can get out of hand, which irritates the Captain.

Zanthoula is alone on watch at 3.30 am on the fourth night when she shakes us awake in some excitement. To port ahead, glistening in moonshine on this darkest of nights, she has sighted the limestone wedge of Tavolara Island, our landmark for the Gulf of Olbia. Together the Captain and I identify the flashes of Tavolara's major light – two long white flashes within a ten-second cycle.

However, with a favourable wind rising, we have every excuse to sail on. There and then we make the decision to aim, not for Sardinia, as first intended, but for Corsica to its north. To this end, we alter course to bring Cape Ferro, the last headland of Sardinia, abeam. Plenty of shipping now demands our attention, not to mention the confusing looms of several lighthouses as we count flashes, ticking off their sources on the chart to position ourselves. Then, up comes Sardinia's most northerly lighthouse, Cape Ferro, three flashes in a fifteen-second cycle.

Shipping is converging on the Bouches de Bonifacio, the channel that divides Sardinia from Corsica, a navigator's nightmare of islands, rocks and reefs, known as a Ships' Graveyard. But, as we work our way past the Maddalena Islands, we encounter no problems. At 8.00 hrs the wind drops. On firing the engine, the Captain finds the exhaust leaking into the engine well "significantly enough to cause concern", as he notes in the log. So now we have a damaged exhaust pipe (again!), a defunct generator and engine vibration sufficient enough to rattle the bones. I might mention that the noise is deafening and that the fumes rival any Hephaestian emission. At least my respiratory system is such that I can breathe a whole lot better than the human beans. At 10.00 am the Captain gets a fix that shows us only 19 miles off Chiappal Point, landmark for the Gulf of Porto Vecchio in Southern Corsica. At 11.00 hrs we hoist the French tricolore.

Girls can be so stupid. As she peers at the Livre de Bord through a pall of smoke, Zanthoula remarks that we shall be "all right now" since Porto Vecchio advertises *"Acceuil aux Handicappés"*. This causes even the hard-pressed Captain a wry smile as he patiently explains to our innocent it means "ramps available for wheelchairs"...but you never know.

Shut in the forepeak all I can do is listen as my Pets prop open the cockpit lockers with whatever they can lay hands on; buckets, saucepans and coils of rope, removing the engine cover and companionway steps to allow free passage of air. Zanthoula, desperate for a cuppa, is devastated when she realises there is little chance of entering the smoke-filled cabin to put the kettle on.

As Miranda's mysterious island rises ahead in all its compelling beauty, my Pets prepare for arrival. Zanthoula's temper takes a dive. (When she gets cross, she gets really cross.) Her blistering resentment in this case is reserved for the happy-go-lucky day sailors cavorting round in their nice clean holiday clothes thinking they know it all, while, under extreme duress, the crew of the Good Ship Cappelle attempt to pick up a buoyed channel by following the inadequate information given in a Livre de Bord they can barely see. A yacht-load of what Zanthoula regards loudly as "smart arses", hearing the noise of Cappelle's engine from half a mile away and presuming power gives way to sail, are in for a rude awakening. Every surface is hot and the vibrations now so severe our bones rattle. It is clear that, once stopped, the engine will be unlikely to start again. Thus, identifying lights, buoys, obstacles and the "Danger de Mort" of the Rock of Chiappino, while avoiding the Banc de Benedetto, we enter the Gulf of Port Vecchio. After an initial mistake – made not by me but corrected by me – at the marina bifurcation marked by red and green buoys, we turn into the marina channel.

Here a French yachtsman waves us towards a vacant slot. Heading in with relief we are caught up short as we run aground. (This slot is for shallow draught only.) But across the way a German yachtsman waits patiently to take our lines. "Saw the smoke!" he calls. St Peter of the Pearly Gates then disappears only to re-materialise carrying in one hand, not a sceptre, but a pack of frozen beer and in the other, not an orb, but a copy of the *New York Times* only three days old. "Welcome to civilisation," he says. (Sometimes thanks are just not enough.)

"I keep watch as Miranda's mysterious island rises ahead in all
its compelling beauty."

TWENTY-THREE

Corsican Interlude

In which we tie up in Corsica.

Golden Boy lets us down.

A garage engineer takes exception to Ship's Cats.

We are now under the French flag. "The cuisine's got to be good," I think, trying out my best paw on Corsican pontoons. No need for recuperative inertia on my part. Zanthoula, on the other hand, detailed by the Captain to tidy up and cheese down the stern warps, is denied R&R until all is Bristol fashion and the sun canopy in place. Quite right too.

Not understanding what a tough life I lead, the French greet me most courteously as an up-market "*chat plaisancier*", and say welcoming things like, *"Relâches-toi, Wackster, mon Vieux! – Bienvenu au Port de Plaisance!"* I know at once I shall enjoy my stay. I also know that the drinking water will be crystalline, since in 1794, Sir Gilbert Elliot, the newly appointed Viceroy, wrote to his wife, Anna Maria, saying that Corsica, which was to become their new home, reminded him of his native Scotland (with a better climate), recommending the drinking water as like "diamonds in solution".

Cappelle is now free to sail French waters for six months before any regulations come into play. You berth where you please. Zanthoula paints her toenails red again and she and the Captain lose no time in settling themselves in basket chairs up in the Citadelle under a green umbrella. Here we lunch on crêpes and grilled prawns threaded on sprigs of rosemary, served with sparkling spring water, followed by French coffee for my Pets. (Later on we get our first taste of Corsica's famous wild boar. No need for stuffing, for these boar feed in the chestnut forests.

A certain stowaway has escaped our minds. But there is to be a sharp reminder of its presence. On Zanthoula opening up the storage compartment under the floorboards, she is aghast to find all our supply of UHT milk dripped away into the bilges through holes gnawed in the corner of each and every waxed carton. It is a desperate discovery. Zanthoula can't live without early tea, with milk. However, on waking next morning she recollects an obscure storage hole in the back of the sink cupboard whose recesses might yet conceal an unviolated carton of Longlife – if you-know-who has not discovered it first. And so it proves!

Sadly, something has to be done, for the Stowaway shows no signs of jumping ship. The crux comes with mouse bites in a fresh bag of brioches the Captain purchases. Since I refuse to take part in the hounding of a fellow live-aboard, I stand by as observer when a high-tech, guaranteed humane mousetrap is procured and primed with best Roquefort. The following morning the trap is sprung, the cheese has vanished – but so has the gourmandising Stowaway. Grimly the Captain resets the trap with Port Salut, adding a square of Belgian chocolate. He then placed the double enticement inside the food locker. Reaching for the marmalade at breakfast next morning, he yelps as his fingers brush the soft body of a very dead (and very pregnant) Aeolian *topo*. (Topo is Italian for "mouse"; it is a nice word.) Her eyes are wide open and she wears a happily anticipatory "cheese AND chocolate. Yum! Yum!" expression, so it seems safe to say she never knew what hit her.

Shampooed and polished, varnished and painted, *Cappelle* looks smart, especially with the addition of the Téte du Maure, the black on white Corsican courtesy flag embellished with the rebel emblem of a Moor's head complete with bandanna. However, our over-riding problem remains the engine, which works on the eternal destruction principle, producing energy in the form of heat and smoke with enough vibration to make your teeth chatter, but insufficient to drive a boat. On taking out a berthing contract, the Captain seeks advice for our problem in the marina office.

At this point, who should enter the scene but Golden Boy, one David. Hearing us reporting an engine problem he comes over from a flotilla to offer his services. (Mind you, I was suspicious from the start. It is not usual for an experienced boat person to clatter on deck in motor-cycle boots. Paws are perfect.) Enough to say, Zanthoula welcomes him with coffee in the mug marked "Admiral". As a start he helps the Captain remove our the alternator (although the Captain does most of the work), vowing to be back with a new one. Should he not be in touch after forty-eight hours he promises to leave a message with the Capitainerie.

Several days go by and we begin to worry in earnest over the non-appearance of Every Mother's Dream. All we get are rumours of him going gadabout to Sardinia on a purloined motorbike. (I don't like motorbikes. When I climb the hill to the Citadelle I have to flatten myself against the wall to keep away from some macho youth executing wheelies on a Yamaha through the narrow Genoese Gate. All part of the Corsican love of dicing with death, they tell me. Safety first is my motto!)

When Golden Boy does at last bounce in with a replacement exhaust my Pets exclaim, "We thought you were DEAD." "So did I," he replies, cheerfully, without explanation. But when we see him again, pasty-faced and pustuled, he is babbling vaguely of "going transatlantic", too stoned to recollect ever having met us. No longer a scion of Michelangelo, he is revealed as Every Mother's Nightmare, just one more on the junkie trail.

Jorgo, a Swiss widower, newly arrived from France, moves in. He has contrived a clever fish trap, which he baits and lowers onto the sea bed overnight. Fond of Ships' Cats, he regularly presents me with a tupperware box layered with gutted and filleted small fry. The larger fish he catches he cooks for himself on a primus stove in his cockpit. The story of Jorgo's fish trap has a sad ending. Some boys with a boat, to whom

Jorgo (to Zanthoula's instinctive disquiet) is seen proudly demonstrating his contraption, steal it one night. The Captain helps him search the sea bed with a magnet the following morning, but the trap has vanished for good and so have the boys and their boat.

In need of gear box repair after his long sail, Jorgo contracts a local garage. It is high time to seek professional help ourselves and the Captain follows suit. When Pierre the Boss and Nico the Sparks turn up they look down their noses at our set-up. (They don't think much of the Ship's Cat either, especially when I catapult through the fore-hatch onto gear they had piled beneath, causing a landslide.)

One morning Zanthoula returns from shopping to find Pierre and Nico wiping their hands on the remains of her Vulcano shirt, which, still smelling alarmingly of bad eggs, had been consigned to the rag bag. The men immediately detail her to get back onto the pontoon to fend off for a test of the new alternator they have fitted. The result is a roar ear-splitting enough to bring the staff rushing out of the Capitainerie, plus a column of black smoke, followed closely by near collision with the pontoon as *Cappelle* surges violently forwards. (Unforgivably, Nico and Sparks have left the engine in gear.) More importantly, Golden Boy's exhaust is reduced to a stinking, smoking heap of rubber as shrivelled as the Wicked Witch in the Wizard of Oz. Pierre, not mincing his words, points out it is not designed for our type of engine (just as, apparently, I am not designed for a ship). Leaving my Pets to clear up the mess, Pierre measures grimly for a replacement.

TWENTY-FOUR

Odysseus Again

In which I embrace the Corsican lifestyle.

We attend a concert and I meet Prospero's daughter.

I suffer another queer turn revealing a further chapter in my past life.

The island's *"dolce far niente"* ways endear me to Corsica. Nothing need be done today that can be done on the morrow. Quite right. How I love sweet nothings. A spot of idleness with your feet up solves most problems. Only on Corsica would one find a notice on a cabin door saying, *"Chut! Maman et bébé dorment!"* I make up my mind to cultivate Corsican ways – and possibly Corsican popsies as well. The girl cats are particularly chic and flirty, even if they are inclined to promote themselves by claiming descent from the Corsican kitten the Emperor Napoleon adopted to comfort him in his exile on St Helena.

One evening I trail my Pets up the winding nursery-rhyme hill to the end-of-season concert in the Eglise de Saint-Jean Bapiste. The doors of the great church stand open wide onto the hot velvet night. Music fills the late summer air. When my Pets enter church, I stretch out in the square under a cork tree. After Paganini's *Campanella* ends, the spotlight falls on a piccolo player, who draws from it the music of Debussy. I have a strong sense that Artemis, Keeper of the Wild Things, is listening with me.

It becomes my habit to trail Zanthoula on her *far niente* expeditions to the Rochers Blancs at the mouth of the estuary. Here I sunbathe on the pillowy white boulders while my Pet slides into the silky waters of the estuary.

One afternoon, as I take a nap in the maquis (heathland), Miranda joins me and sits down to talk. She is not the "silly, love-sick little goose" her father, Prospero, thinks her, but a lovely, friendly girl who likes cats. As a magician and rightful Duke of Milan, her father, Prospero, had, in times past, engineered a fearsome tempest to bring his usurping brother Antonio, together with his own friend, King Alonso of Naples, to the island where he would entrap them by a shipwreck of his making and sort the matter of succession out once and for all. I know the ending to the story: Prospero's magic restored him to his rightful inheritance, Miranda married her boyfriend Ferdinand, Alonso's son, and they all lived happily ever after. When I awake, Miranda has wandered off and is gathering arbutus blossoms in her bunched skirts.

I make up my mind to spend more time, not only in keeping up my diary, but out and about. I have many friends in the marina – although I do admit to once having been mistaken for a feral cat and thrown off a super-yacht. (Could they not see I am of a superior class?) On *Tiger Shark*, on the other hand, another luxury craft, I am made welcome by the captain's wife, who encourages me to loll on her sun deck and share the sofa in her sun lounge. My elevation from *gamin de rochers* (alley cat) to *chat plaisancier* (marina cat) on a super-yacht suits my style fine. It is far too good an invitation to pass over In fact I spend so much time on *Tiger Shark* the captain's wife presents Zanthoula with a tulle poke of sugared almonds from her daughter's wedding in Paris in token appreciation of the loan of her Ship's Cat.

Sometimes my escapades are reported to my Pets. I am noted of an evening, trotting down the main concourse towards the flowerbeds where the humming-bird hawk moths vibrate. From here my date-of-the-night and I will high tail it off to some quality restaurant to be nice to its clients.

When Pierre next appears he is bearing a Peugeot exhaust which he proposes to cut in half. His mood is aggressive. He is a motor, not a marine engineer, fast taking exception to boats (as well as Ships' Cats), he says. The exhaust is cut, fitted and gummed in record time, but disaster strikes again when the engine is taken to 3,000 revs, at which point the accelerator cable sticks. The resultant jerk yanks the ship-to-shore electricity cable out of its housing. With the accelerator jammed, a roar like that of a thousand aero engines shakes the mountains. Again, the staff burst forth from the Capitainerie, this time fearing an earthquake. Pierre bellows that not only is *Cappelle's* previous owner a *charlatan*, but anyone acquiring her (and her Ship's Cat!) is a *pigeon*. With this he leaves, threatening to return for immediate cash payment. Jorgo, who was keeping a close eye on proceedings on *Cappelle*, at once moves forward to commiserate and bring us the special *ratatouille* he has created for our lunch, saying that Pierre, while failing to finish the job and demanding cash payment had likewise walked out on Mojo.

Jorgo is not our only good neighbour, for the crew of *Pat's Girl*, a Nantucket Clipper, vie for my attention with the flying fish that land on her deck. They get into the habit of lobbing them over to me and later send a photograph from France of me fielding a flying fish..

When at last we are free to continue our odyssey, my Pets set about steering a trolley of canisters of cut-price fuel back from the supermarket garage down the edge of the fast Route de la Douane, as is the dangerous but accepted practice of live-aboards. But then the weather breaks. We scarce have time to fasten on boat covers before thunder rolls along the hills like wagon trains and *Cappelle* shudders under reverberating sonic claps and slashing downpours while I retreat behind the water tank. Storm after storm advances and recedes, rainbow dervishes dancing around the mast until astonishing visibility returns to reveal an awesome land-scape unfurling in ragged vistas of granite pyramids. To the south, towards Sardinia, flickers of lightning light up a baroque cloud from within one evening, as if it were a sunset pink lampshade over a faulty light bulb. On a rare night of calm we take our sundowners in the cockpit, where I exquisitely rub my face in Zanthoula's dish of olives on the table. (I find their aroma intoxicating.) From somewhere a yachtsman serenades us with his trumpet. You could have heard a pin drop in the marina.

Our next destination is the south of France. When passage-planning to or from Corsica we need to remember that a twenty-four-hour weather window is a prerequisite. Since it is already the third week in September, a mistral, an "impetuous and terrible wind", that fans out from the Rhône delta, is a likely hazard. We must keep a listening watch at all times. With weather warnings out for an *aggravation importante*, plus a *perturbation intéréssante* not to mention a *houle* (gale), we fill in time with a visit to Bonifacio on the far side of the island, an ancient town set on the brink of a *calanque*, a mile-long slit in limestone cliffs.

As soon as we enter the creek I suffer a dizzy spell. "What's the matter with him?" enquires Zanthoula. When my vision clears, I find myself once again Ship's Cat on Odysseus's Ship-of-No-Name, this time supervising the placing of a great stone anchor in the Calanque de l'Arenella, described by Homer as "a curious bay with mountain walls of stone to left and right" where Odysseus is sheltering his fleet.

As *Cappelle* presses on into the depths of this dramatic hurricane hole, Zanthoula is glad to see me recovering from my fainting fit.

But, sure enough, it happens again. Once more I am back as Ship's Cat on the mighty trireme where Odysseus is busy dispatching sailors to make contact with the locals. For a closer view of the cliffs, scarred like millefeuilles, instinct leads me to spring onto the trireme's bows. My breath catches as I glimpse a band of wild men with cudgels up on the cliffs. Our sailors are out of luck, for the Laestrygonians, a fearsome tribe of man-eating giants, are waiting in ambush. Hurling down rocks on Odysseus's fleet, they destroy all but our flagship, the Ship-of-No-Name, strategically placed by Odysseus at the entrance to the *calanque*. We are lucky to escape with our lives. Others less fortunate are torn to pieces by tribesmen or harpooned "like fish" and carried off for supper. Their cries ring in my head, as I jerk back to the present to find myself back home on *Cappelle*.

With Special Weather Warning No 83 Vents de Vent Fort from Toulon posted outside the Capitainerie and the weather stormy around Cap Corse, Corsica's northerly tip, it remains unwise to leave the shelter of Porto Vecchio. Then the newspapers break news of an oil slick around the Cap. Inspected from the air, this is identified as a thick mat of seaweed, which should clear.

We pay close attention to the skies, local law having it that on the evening preceding a mistral the sunset is exceptionally red with cigar-shaped clouds, at first red and then turning grey, the faster the transformation the stronger the mistral. According to tradition, the mistral blows in multiples of three, six or nine days, although it can blow for anything from one to twelve days. When it does blow, the sky becomes gas-jet blue with an unreal, electric quality.

Before we leave Porto Vecchio, Yorgo makes sure our pressure pot is stacked with herb-dowsed steaks of wild boar nourished on chestnuts and wild cyclamen root – and that there is a special box of filleted small fry for me.

TWENTY-FIVE

We Cross to France

In which we enter the Ligurian Sea.

We encounter a sperm whale.

When Zanthoula sails recklessly, the Captain and I save the
day.

In early October, with a forecast of stable weather, we set off on
overnight sail to Maccinaggio, eighty nautical miles north, last harbour
before Cap Corse. First to malfunction is the rev counter – and that
is before we exit the Gulf. Abeam Percorella beacon the Captain and I
stream the Walker log, changing course to four miles off shore. I am
sorely tempted to pounce when a wren flies aboard, but it clings too high
on the shrouds to reach and makes off towards Solenzara at its third
attempt. What is it doing so far from land?

Our progress is orderly, though care has to be taken due to magnetic
variations of up to five degrees. Nonetheless, Zanthoula cooks wild
boar steaks for supper. This is followed by rice pudding garnished with
rum and chestnut purée. (I savour EVERYTHING.) Sketched against a
sky turning pale, the 4,000 ft rock needles of the Col de Bavella cleave
the air. We duck instinctively when starry trajectories burst from the
stelliferous skies above, threatening to explode on our heads.

At midnight we take our position from the Alistro light (2 flash / 10
sec cycle), changing course due north, to sail alongside La Castagniccia,

Corsica's celebrated chestnut forest, grazing ground of the wild boar and an area riddled with magic. Here we haul in the Walker log to free it of a plastic bag. Then Zanthoula and I stand watch.

> Be not afeared, the isle is full of noises,
> Sounds and sweet airs.

Old people still heed these voices, especially on All Hallows Eve, in a belief that the dead inspire wise decisions. Several different types of witchcraft flourished here, long-drawn-out duels with asphodel cudgels being fought out between black witches and white witches, who might, *mirabile dictu*, operate as both. Born black and white and descended via broomstick, I am tailor-made for witchcraft, one might say. I am also beginning to think I shall be glad to leave this region of Dream Hunters and Bilocators (a sort of Higgs boson people with the ability to appear in two places at once), especially now that Halloween is approaching.

In the clarity of the atmosphere the illuminated coastline, although four to six miles distant, looms all too close, causing us to miss several heartbeats when a cruise liner the size of the Parthenon passes by on our inside to enter Bastia. At 05.00 hrs the Captain takes over the helm. Three hours later we are abeam Macinaggio on the island's northern scut. Now that we are approaching Cap Corse, the sea develops an unpleasant chop, reminding us that, whatever the forecast, we must prepare for winds of forty kts, with confused seas, around the Cap.

But now the wind is favourable and with one accord we know the answer, for:

> "Fair stands the wind for France
> When we our sails advance
> Nor now to prove our chance
> Longer will tarry."

It is farewell to Corsica. On the rocky Isles Finocchiarola lies a wrecked coaster. Taking a chance on the shallows between Cap Corse and the steep-to Ile de la Giraglia with its mighty lighthouse, we steal a march on a pair of yachts out of Macinaggio to emerge into the Ligurian Sea as leader of the pack.

But Nemesis, daughter of Oceanus issues due warning for, on changing helm, we gybe all standing. I brace myself with all four feet. Too busy to argue, we are soon goose-winging across the white caps at five kts, the wind E S/E, Force 5, into the beautiful uncertainty that lies ahead, while the craggy coronet of Corsica sinks slowly into the wastes behind. Corsica has allure and I will its dramatic peaks not to abandon us too soon. In the distance, the white flame of its sail nicking the horizon, a yacht is fixed on our course.

Suddenly something dramatic occurs. I am down in the galley keeping an eye on the wild boar soup when I hear the Captain gasp. Leaping up the steps, I am just in time to see a huge blunt head burst from the swirling water at our side. It is a sperm whale, the size of which makes me more than ever glad to have clung on when we gybed. A few bulls and some cows are known to have retired from the Atlantic to the deep waters off Corsica. When the monster dives, leaving turbulent seas, the flukes of its magnificent tail seem as wide as the wings of an aircraft.

The October days are short. By 15.30 hrs the air is cooling rapidly as we sail westward on a gold-flecked sea straight for the pimento globe of the sun, soon to be replaced by the moon's silver apple. When Hesperus, the Evening Star emerges, the yacht on our tail is still following. But then darkness falls and "She sinks into the moonlight / and the sea is only sea." We miss her company.

We have been sailing strongly for seven hours. Then the wind drops. By the time Zanthoula and I take the midnight watch, it has picked up again. Zanthoula is jubilant about our progress, so much so that she puts me "before the mast", i.e. in the forepeak. Thinking of the sperm whale, I don't argue, and it must be admitted we are rollicking about a bit. I also get the feeling that Zanthoula's mood is over the top. Fizzing with false confidence, she won't take any advice from me.

The Captain sleeps while we romp downwind under full main with the genoa pulled out. I can feel *Cappelle* surfing, her stern lifting to the wave behind so that she shoots down its slope. A yacht needs a sail that's obliquely set, otherwise she threatens to gybe, bringing the "widow-maker" (aka the boom) over with a crash. As I am flung about in the forepeak, I am fearful Zanthoula has forgotten *Cappelle* is not a square-rigger. With their yards not set precisely square, the old galleons thrived on wind from astern. A Bermudan sloop behaves differently.

Changing course five miles nearer the Italian Riviera to pick up the west-flowing current only makes for added impetus. "**MEE-OW-OW-OW! MEE-OW-OW-OW!**" I howl in an attempt to alert the Captain, but he cannot hear me. Sometimes I catch intermittent glimpses of the translucent caps of waves, as they turn pretty pink or grassy green according to whether they catch the reflection from our port or starboard light as it swings crazily about on broken water during the yacht's unpredictable roll. I know what Zanthoula is doing. She is relying on speed to keep us out of trouble and deliver us to our destination in record time. I know the feeling. There is a moment when a boat feels big and invincible, as if her power derives from within and not from the cold-hearted seas behind. I pray Zanthoula will recognise *Cappelle,* with her precious cargo, for what she is – small and vulnerable – before it is too late.

But, in an effort to make landfall before dark the following day, careering along on a madcap fairground ride, Zanthoula sticks with it. Going with wind and sea gives an illusion of unity, but can be dangerous. What am I to do? *Cappelle* cants steeply, water sluicing across her deck. As the yacht dips and dives, I am only too well aware, in my own uncomfortable confinement, of what is going on. But Zanthoula, who is relying on a well-designed boat always righting herself, continues to succumb to deceptive influences. I grow desperate. At midnight we are still riding the crests of peruked waves when I hear the unmistakable sound of a breaker slapping Zanthoula in the back. Abandoning the helm, she stumbles into the cabin to shake the Captain out of his coma and switch on the chart light. Am I relieved.

But it isn't over yet. "We're on course and GOING REALLY FAST!" Zanthoula announces cheerfully. At this the Captain awakes to the yacht's unpredictable roll and leaps into the cockpit. All hell breaks loose. "What the blazes do you think you are doing? Are you deaf or something? Can't you HEAR the wind? Can't you SEE what's going on? For CHRISSAKE! Something's GONNA BREAK!" There's a lot more unsuitable to record and even more frantic "**MEE-OW!-OW!-OWING!**" from me.

From being drunk on elation, Zanthoula sobers up sharply. How could she not have heard the devilish caterwauling of the wind (a sort of high-pitched scream) in the rigging or my frantic protests!

The Captain's first task is to pull in the mainsail. Then he recovers the boathook that poles out the genoa. This is so tightly lashed with wet cord that it takes long, colourful moments to free one end, only to have it snatched from his hand. As *Cappelle* starts on the opposite roll, he grabs the boathook, binding it to the guardrail as it threatens to stab him in the eye. Then he heaves to, ties the wheel and fires the engine to hold us steady. While Zanthoula winds in the genoa, he releases the sheet. Under Captain's orders to take the helm again, Zanthoula unties the cord securing the gear lever and struggles to gain control when the helm is liberated. It is then that I am let me out to lend assistance in taking the yacht round 180 degrees up into wind to face the way we came so that the mainsail may be successfully reefed.

Meanwhile, the Captain is sprawled supine on the coach-roof endeavouring to tie reefing points by trial and error finger-touch, it being too dark to distinguish the lines by their red and green flecks. If Zanthoula fails to hold *Cappelle* directly into wind, the mainsail fills, shifting strongly to one side or the other like a mad umbrella, making the Captain's task of yanking down and securing reefing points impossible. To prevent the boom taking a swipe at him, Zanthoula clings to the helm with her left arm, while clutching both the helm and the mainsheet with her right. Since the tell-tales are impossible to see, I get tears in my eyes and a crick in my neck as I strain to keep an eye on the wind vane so that Zanthoula can hold the boat true. At last the Captain gets in a surprisingly tidy reef and raises the mainsail. We are back in business.

Our first task is to return on course. With the Captain shining a torch on the binnacle, Zanthoula hauls *Cappelle* around to port, holding her on 260 degrees, south of west, so that the Captain can reset the runners with a muffled hammer and winch out a small jib. A few stars peep. Making sure to feel the wind on her starboard cheek, Zanthoula chooses the brightest as a fix. With the preventer needing to be reset, the Captain goes forward. "Keep an eye on that freighter behind you," he yells from the foredeck. (I had already seen it, of course.) Unfortunately, as she glances over her shoulder, Zanthoula lets *Cappelle* gybe. "CONCENTRATE, CAN'T YOU," bawls the Captain above the roar of the wind.

Something then comes over Zanthoula and me, not panic but a mind-sharpening anger, excellent for sea-management. "How dare that freighter give us grief. Let her look after herself." The chests of a re-born Cabin Boy and a Ship's Cat-with-Attitude swell. (You start by making a voyage and end with the voyage making you.) "Do your stuff, Wackster!" calls Zanthoula, while muttering to herself, "Come on, Horatia Hornblower, forget about Davy Jones Locker, JUST SAIL THIS BOAT." On we speed, decisively, with confidence, bang on course, red blood coursing through our veins. I am not Ship's Cat on this yacht for nothing.

Quite suddenly, after little more than two hours and the loss of three or four sea miles, *Cappelle*, on course 260 degs, sails balanced, making five kts, one reef in the main, half a genoa, engine off, wind abating, sea calming, crosses into another world.

TWENTY-SIX

A Shadow Overhangs

In which we tie up on the Côte d'Azur.
Zanthoula becomes a lavender addict and buys books.
We refurbish the mast. Quarantine for me is discussed.

We gulp down water while the Captain congratulates Zanthoula on grabbing his towelling scarf as it flew over her head. I am commiserated with for having deposited a mixture of wild boar and rice pudding on the carpet. (It was my very first bout of seasickness. I suspect it was the rum that did it.)

In the light of a new day, a coast-seeking current driving us north, we are back on 270 deg, due west. An hour later I whoop, "**WHEE! LOOK-E-E! SEE-E-E!**" Forward and to starboard rises a magnificent lighthouse crowning a bold wooded cape. It has to be Cap Camarat. "**VIVE LA FRANCE! SALUT! SALUT! VIVE LA BELLE FRANCE!**" we yell, toasting land-ahoy in mugs of tea and cat biscuits, with cheers for *Cappelle* and hugs for one another.

Then doubt set in. For, although the Pilot informs us (in its usual casual way) that Cap Camarat is "easily recognised", what we take to be the lighthouse's old signal station appears on the wrong side of the building and the "conspic" girder tower is missing. Either the photograph showing a misleading view of the lighthouse from our direction of approach is the wrong way round (which turns out to be the case), or it is the wrong lighthouse. But after an hour's closing approach the problem is solved when I give a triumphant ear-splitter, "**LOOK AT THESE ROCKS! WORRA-WORRA-WORRA!!**" on recognising a line of them extending outwards. These have to be the Roches Fourasi off Cap Taillat.

Cappelle has made it to the South of France.

Late October or not, day sailers potter about on a bubble blue sea in the balmy air of the Côte d'Azur. Here we are just sailing along on a late summer's day. How cool. Suddenly we are as fresh as daisies. Should we make Porquerolles in the Isles of Gold our destination? Or Cavalaire-sur-Mer on the mainland? Since it is the nearest resort to St Tropez, Zanthoula chooses Cavalaire. All we have to do now, after rescuing the Walker log spinner from trouble ahead, is to negotiate a wind-row of junk-laden vegetation and tree roots spreading out from the mainland.

Two hundred and eight nautical miles from Porto Vecchio we tie up on Cavalaire's Quai d'Acceuil. All is quiet in the laid-back afternoon. *Toujours* on the button, I go off to present myself to the natives and see what I can see. "*Ça va! Big Boy!*" they say, in Italian-accented provençal.

That night we dine on rabbits' thighs from a rotisserie and listen to smoochy music on Radio Nostalgie. It is *collapsez-vous* time. At last our muscles can sign off. Later that night gales and heavy showers catch up with us, which necessitates my waking Zanthoula in the early hours to give me a rub-down with my special towel.

Zanthoula, suitably attired as she sees fit in a striped matelot shirt and espadrilles, dons her battered straw hat and makes haste to establish the Taste of Provence. Not just the taste of it, but the scents too. *Sarriette* and *romarin* (savory and rosemary) replace Greek herbs. Then she goes bonkers on lavender.

> "Here's flowers for you;
> Hot lavender, mints, savory, marjoram..."

just like in *The Winter's Tale*.

It was the Romans who introduced lavender to Provence, planting it in their vineyards to add aroma to their wine. The more I sniff lavender, the more I love it – it beats diesel any time. It is my happiness smell. When Zanthoula buys lavender honey in the farmers' market its scent fills the cabin as she opens a jar. She puts lavender bags under our pillows, sticks lavender bouchons in the wine bottles and even buys soap and loo paper *à la lavande*. (She does go over the top sometimes.)

October degenerates into a volatile month of sunshine interrupted by strong winds and black squalls bagged with rain. Soon snow lies on the medium heights, with a chance of the canals freezing over. Then comes the *évolution* of a strong south easterly. The spume-filled sea lacks horizon, melding with the sky. When a Force 8 / 10 Vent d'Est sweeps in, it traps a sand-burdened cloud against the Pradels, the collar of hills behind Cavalaire. As the wind drops, down comes the rain, blasting us with Saharan sand (which some call "Gaddafi dust" and others "blood rain"). When the storm blows out it leaves the air full of red-bellied dragonflies.

It is the Captain's intention to sail on to Port St Louis, port of entry for the River Rhône, but the weather soon lets us know we are better off where we are. Cavalaire might give a forlorn impression out of season, but we are made welcome in the back streets. Zanthoula buys "*Pourquoi je t'aime*" cat food. She also discovers a bookshop and makes friends with the little old lady who sells traditional crib figurines called *santon*s made of *terre cuite*. Each time Zanthoula buys a *santon* to add to her Christmas crib collection the old lady gives her a lavender bag to go with it.

One day Zanthoula purchases a book about a girl called Manon, who skips in the garrigues (similar to the Corsican maquis). She also buys one for me called *French for Cats* by Henri de la Barbe. Of course, I already communicate in French but there remains room for improvement. Now whenever I take *un petit somme* (a little nap) I rest my head on Henri de la Barbe to absorb its learning. When I sit in front of my blue bowl, I have taught myself to say, "*Je veux qu'on remplisse mon bol!*" It doesn't make Zanthoula fill it up any quicker (even when I add "*Immédiatement, s'il vous plait),* it just proves I'm integrating.

Believe you me, French polish serves me well with the mamselles who live in the rocks. As Françoise Hardy sang, "*Tous les garçons et les filles de mon âge / Se promènent dans la rue deux par deux*". That goes for cats too. I am considered a splendid "*matou*" – *haut bohême* style. Another book Zanthoula buys me is *Rendez-moi Mes Poux* ("Bring Me Back My Fleas") about a little French boy who loves to play Tiddly Winks with his fleas and fiercely resents their banishment. (I am always thankful to be rid of mine.)

One day a powerful thunderclap drives me behind the water tank. When the summits of the Pradels re-emerge they are wearing aprons of mist round their midriffs. The sky beyond is ink black. As we raise our voices in defiance of the blow, Cavalaire's Heavy Weather Sailing School rockets out of harbour to meet Severe Gale Force 9. Meanwhile the Captain, sheltered by the cockpit cover propped up with an oar, commits himself to a problem beneath the swan neck of the exhaust system.

Gale warnings, accompanied by heavy rain, are frequently posted for the Littoral Varois. On a wintry Toussaint (All Saints' Day) we awake to strident music, all part of the Capitainerie's official welcome to the Student World Cup. The weather is foul and the crews, carelessly chucking their empty take-away trays, beer cans and bottles onto the pontoons fail to endear themselves to us live-aboards left to clear up the mess. Several competing yachts retire, one with the Stars & Stripes, together with a tattered Irish flag, wrapped round the stump of its shattered mast. The local newspaper describes the race as held under a black sky "*qui ressemblait plus à celui du Cap Horn en plein tourmante*" (more like Cape Horn in a full gale) than the skies of the regattas normally fought out in the Mediterranean.

When the wind fails to blow hard enough to tear the ears off a donkey, as they say in the Midi, the Captain leaps to his feet with the words, "*On va attaquer le mât!*" His aim is to refurbish our mast. I do not relish this unnecessary project. Could we not have a bit of rest and relaxation instead? It is my job to support the Captain and, let's face it, he might drop something on me. I could end up flatter than a *crêpe suzette*. Needless to say, on the Captain's instructions, we help fashion a bosun's chair from an offcut of wood, while poor Zanthoula is detailed to winch thirteen stone of him she holds most dear up the mast on rope pulleys while juggling a lifeline and rope stirrup at the same time. I, albeit rather nervously, volunteer to man the foot of the mast to keep an eye on things. (Should the Captain need me I could shin up it a lot faster than he can in his makeshift contraption.)

Mine is not the healthiest of spots. Twice a day, weather permitting, with midday break, we set to. On the fourth day, quite without warning, the main halyard, which Zanthoula and I are enjoined to keep an eye on to make sure it does not jam in its spool on the open-drive winch, snaps with a loud report, surrounding us with whipping coils of steel cable. At almost the same moment the feet of the Captain, fortunately not too far elevated, hit the deck with a bang – missing me by a hair's breadth. (I should get danger money.) Supplied and fitted by "the best rigger in Lavrion" the halyard is then exposed as not solid at all but filled with rotting cotton fibre. Later on, I run up the mast to inspect what we call "the bullet hole" (really a knot hole in the wood). It is gratifying when re-varnishing brings cries of "*Quel joli mât!*" from the French. That night a glorious Hunter's Moon shines on our handiwork as I go about my feline affairs in the golden dark.

I am happy in Cavalaire. There is much of interest. Moreover, I have conveniently taken over the geranium bed in front of the Marina Bar as my loo – the "NO DOGS!" sign not applying. But I am also aware of serious discussions taking place over the cabin table about what is to happen next. There are various possibilities, apparently. The canal route home has been vetoed by the French, who declare it "*Tout à fait impossible!*" for *Cappelle* on account of her deep draught. She will bog down in the mud, they insist. (A pity. Shore leave, canal-side, could be fun.) Additionally, we are advised against passage of the River Rhône because of the strength of its current. A pity again. I fancy dancing "Sur le Pont d'Avignon" (to Scott Joplin's *Elite Syncopation,* perhaps) on the original Pont d'Avignon.

In all discussions an alarming new word looms – "quarantine" – disagreeable apparently, but inevitable, since I am destined to travel to England. Quarantine is a rabies preventative that lasts a long time – six whole months of my life. At worst it is prison, at best it is house arrest – but it is nonetheless forced confinement. Besides, none of us relishes the idea of separation.)

We at least expect to sail home to England together. But even that idea is quashed. as I shall only be allowed to sail as far as the three-mile limit, from which, incurring vast expense, a licensed quarantine carrier must put out to collect me. It is finally decided I should fly home to start my "penance" early, so that I may join my ship again in six months' time when it reaches English shores. ("If it ever does, without my assistance," I opine distractedly.)

TWENTY-SEVEN

I Leave Solo on a Big Adventure

Zanthoula makes a friend. I am wary of the dog Jacomo.

Zanthoula and I survive a mistral.

I fly off to quarantine.

In the stillness of dawn, while filaments of blue wood smoke rise lazily from the cottage chimneys on the Pradels, we move to winter quarters in a shared berth in the corner of the main concourse. *Cappelle's* companion is *Minnehaha*, a canoe-stern Colin Archer skippered by a Princess Anne lookalike. (More anon about my encounters with the real Princess Anne, would you believe?) Hailing from north Germany "where the sun never shines", Anna, a bachelor girl, loves *Minnehaha* so much she has bought her a *foulque*, a decoy coot, as a pet, attaching it to her stern with a length of string.

Though Zanthoula and Anna get on well, I am wary, for Anna has a boon companion, Jacomo, a rescue German Shepherd, whom nobody trusts, not even Anna. (He once pinned her down in her own cabin.) Anna arrives every morning from her camper van on the digue on a bicycle festooned with laundry, then spends the day working on boat matters on a Black & Decker worktable she sets up on the quay, Jacomo (who is never fed red meat) tethered beside her with a bowl of water. As long as I do not venture within striking distance of that tether (which I pray never breaks), I reckon I'll be OK.

Mel has been tasked with seeking out suitable quarantine kennels for me in England. Blessings be upon her for those she chooses! Wey Farm is described as "the ultimate in cat care with the very latest refinements in luxury service for felines". It is clear to me on arrival that it is no ordinary establishment, but strictly for Top Cats! A log fir burns in the spacious reception lounge, while on the mantelpiece stands a framed letter from Her Majesty the Queen (no less) expressing her appreciation for the care taken of her dogs. It is true I am to be detained in quarantine at Her Majesty's pleasure, but it seems Wey Farm does truly afford Her Majesty pleasure, for she entrusts her own animals to its care. (Is it the corgis?)

As requested by Wey Farm, Mel duly submits my dietary requirements, personal preferences, likes and dislikes as to grooming, nail-clipping, teeth-cleaning, handling, other animals and people, together with a comprehensive Personality Profile. (This is so that Wey Farm can make me feel as much at home as possible.) Mel also completes and signs Booking Form C3 on my behalf and applies for an Import Licence from the Min of Ag & Fish. According to the requirements of the said MAFF (Ministry of Agriculture, Fisheries & Food) Rabies Order, there are arrangements to finalise at the French end. I accordingly pay several visits to my travel agent in Cavalaire, an exquisite young woman of Mediterranean appearance. Alabaster-skinned, narrow-featured, with arched eyebrows, she deserves to be serenaded by troubadours and to wear a pointy hat. It is clear a pair of gaze hounds with seed pearl collars should attend her, rather than a questionable tomcat like me. But I am her "*petit chat*" and she is devoted to me. (On reaching England the first thing I do is to send her a Christmas card.)

We believe I might fly home to England with Zanthoula, but the answer from both British Airways and Air France is "*Non! – absolutment catégorique*" (a favourite phrase among the French). From Nice Airport I must travel freight (?!!) to Heathrow in an IATA approved, paw-proof and nose-proof *Pet Voyageur* of regulation dimensions. This is to be obtained via my vet in Cavalaire – in fact he gives me the one he bought for his daughter's kitten and throws in free *pis-pis* pads. It is essential that my *Pet Voyageur* bears the all-important *etiquette rouge*, or "Red Ticket", supplied by MAFF.

Finally, a quotation of £100 for the taxi fare to deliver me to Nice Airport led my Pets to decide it worthwhile for the Captain to fetch our car from England. It could then be used both to ferry me to Nice and them home for Christmas. Gale warnings were out when Zanthoula and I saw the Captain off to London one dark and blustery morning to fetch the car and collect my *etiquette rouge*. Little did Zanthoula and I guess the experience that lay ahead!

That day the barometer plummeted to 993 millibars. Later the weather warning *"Avis de coup de vent N/W (Mistral) Sector, Menance de 50 noeuds"* is displayed outside the Capitainerie and the air blows increasingly cold. Then a further bulletin *"Menace de 55 noeuds"* ("Threat of 55 knots") is posted. All is mellow lamplight in the cabin when Zanthoula returns from watching a wedding party leave the *Mairie*, rose petals and rice mixing with the swirl of autumn leaves. I am curled up on the Captain's berth ready for teatime when Zanthoula lays out her *santons* to drool over.

We are aware that the wind is rising, but the wrap-around warmth (and false security) of the cabin divorces us from its influence. Even when the hull rocks and the updating weather bulletin describe the blow as *"très fort à violent"*, I refuse to be concerned until I hear the words, *"Avis de tempête!"* ("Storm warning!") On going on deck I find the gusting wind doing its best to turn my ears inside out. Moreover, at the core of each lull I think I detect a sinister, faraway, dynamo whine.

Beyond a certain velocity, the mistral takes on a persona, creating a relationship with those that lie in its path as of pursuer and pursued. Seeking out, it lies in wait for the optimum moment to pounce. The longer the mistral lasts, the more paranoia it engenders and the more self-control frays. Remissions come as pregnant pauses. My sensitive ears pick up a thin bat's cry that grows increasingly persistent as it descends to decibels audible to human ears and a *rafale* (squall) roars in.

The ear-blocking maw of noise sucks away the oxygen and leaves me fighting for breath. I know it! The Furies (otherwise known as the Triple Hecate or the Three Erinnyes) are clawing their way through the air waves on direct approach to *Cappelle*. It is ME these bat-winged crones with brass snakes for hair (known in France as *"Les Bonnes Dames Charitables"* or "the Kindly Ones") are out to get. It is unwise to speak their name out loud, for this could tempt fate. To "diss" them brings down vengeance. They might order me to bite off my tail in sacrifice, just as they ordered storm-bound sailors to bite off a finger. It is too much. I can stand it no longer! Crouched on my belly, I reach the hatch and catapult down into the cabin.

Zanthoula, after lashing the forepeak doors and tying down the lamp, whose bulb has split, grabs our vase of flowers and tries to weave some sort of crown of lilies – part of the traditional ritual to appease The Furies. (She swears she is not doing anything of the sort, but I don't believe her.) Suddenly something much weightier than a chaplet of *fleurs de lys* clouts her on the cheek as the ship's clock flies off the wall. Scrabbling up the curtains (a nervous reaction, aimed at achieving maximum elevation), I am engulfed by a double-sided landslip, as the contents of the cabin avalanche on top of me, first from one side and then the other, while the ship cants at an angle of forty-five degrees before staggering back to tip the other way, rocking violently. Then the kettle empties itself on my head. I must say that at this point I quite lose my imperturbability and wail piteously, "**MEE-OW!, MEE-OW! MEE-OW-OW-OW!**

The ferocity of the wind penetrates every seam in *Cappelle* as the Furies mark us. The next four hours, as we await daylight, are the longest ever. Zanthoula drags me out from under a heap of radio, cushions, plastic wine glasses, mugs, bowls of fruit, cups, plates, saucers, books and charts. Everything that isn't on top of me, or on the floor, or on our berths, has landed on the cooker, or in the sink. Zanthoula clears what space she can of assorted impedimenta and we clutch each other fearfully to await events.

Nothing worse happens until, at long last, the black night turns into a dirty grey dawn. The wind remains strong but the gusts are lessening so Zanthoula crawls outside on her knees and lies flat, dragging herself along the deck on her elbows, me belly-crawling with her. The stern warp protectors have jolted off. To Zanthoula's mind, if they part, we will collide with *Minnehaha* and throw her against the quay. However, *Minnehaha* seems in fairly good order, her rubber snubbers lengthening and shortening as she plays the onslaught. Dimly I can see Anna keeping watch from the doorway of the marina office. At midnight, we learn, she and Jacomo attempt to reach the marina, but Jacomo is blown off his feet and she off her bike. They then return, with difficulty, to her van from which she makes it to the marina alone, on foot, via a back way, in the shelter of buildings.

Zanthoula slithers back to a cockpit locker for the spare anchor warp, hoping somehow to use it for reinforcement. Having secured one end to the windlass, if she gets her timing right, she might make it onto the pontoon to fasten the other end. This proves impossible. She then makes determined efforts, lying flat, to lasso a water hydrant, eventually succeeding, but at the next gust the hydrant starts to pull away and she lets go. By this time yacht owners are arriving. Zanthoula calls out to a passing Frenchman who, summing up our situation in a flash, catches the anchor warp she throws him, wraps it round a bollard and, without so much as a word or a glance at either of us, leaps aboard to cleat the warp in a figure-of-eight round the base of our mast and windlass and then leaps off again on his way to assess his own damage.

That was all there is to it, really. According to the *Var Matin*, though "*froid et fort*" and reaching hurricane-force, the mistral had been a sprint rather than a marathon. The palm trees, winterised with swaddling bands, polythene night-caps over their top-knots, have mostly survived. *Cappelle*'s severe heel is explained, the Port Captain says, by us having picked up the wrong lazy line, thus angling the yacht to the wind.

Putting *Cappelle* to rights, including cheesing down in the prescribed manner, takes until midday. After which Zanthoula fills hot-water bottles and we snuggle under the duvet, waking only to share a *trempête*, a baguette dipped in broth made from last night's leftover lamb stew. Then we both sleep soundly until the following morning.

Trying to appear both unconcerned and in earnest, Zanthoula, goes to telephone the Captain in London to ask him to bring back rubber snubbers, or at least a supply of super strong warp. In perfect weather we picnic in the cockpit on the alert for a red Alfa Romeo. (Of course, not so much as a breeze stirs in the clear blue sky.)

"What mistral?" queries the Captain, surveying the tranquil scene while frowning at Zanthoula's cat's cradle of warp around the windlass, which she has not dared undo. (It is plain the Little Woman panicked.) Anna, giving ear from *Minnehaha*, immediately steps forward in our support, telling him strong men had been unnerved by such a blow as we survived. Even then he remains curiously unmoved. He has brought some extra warp, but no snubbers. "Men," snorts Anna. "They're all the same."

The Captain has with him my all-important *etiquette rouge*. My first outing – not a success in my opinion – in my *Pet Voyageur* is to the vet to obtain a "*Certificat Sanitaire*" for a small animal in transit. My next visit is to the Lady Rosamunde to confirm my travel arrangements: Air Azur ETD 12.45 hrs Nice-Heathrow on 27th November. After that there is nothing to do but face the inevitable.

I howl all the way down the motorway, "**H-E-E-E-L-P MEE NOW-OW-OW!**" The traffic's roar is too much for my frayed nerves. Even worse are the gigantic figures of Grand Guignol speed cops, coloured a terrifying bright orange, spaced out along the Nice autoroute waving mechanical arms. One glimpse at a gesticulating metal arm is enough to make me throw up. ("Oh Wacky, do you have to?" says Zanthoula.) At the Zone Fret the Captain signs the last of the documentation consigning five kilos of two-year-old black and white cat, *chatré* (neutered), measuring fifty-two cm *sans queue* (without tail), to Martini Technotrans SA, his flight to Heathrow, and Fate. Then comes the moment to say goodbye. A miserable whimper is the only answer I can muster to farewells that tear at the heart strings.

However, it doesn't turn out so badly after all – although it is true I do not relish solitary confinement. I enjoy being a five-star Top Cat all right! No wonder Her Majesty is pleased with the service at Wey Farm. We cats have our own kitchen where fresh food is prepared and cooked to suit our personal tastes. Each of us has our own individual two-floor chalet with electrically heated cat basket, plus ramp and climbing platform complete with artificial grass. In the circumstances we want for nothing. Wey Farm is even thoughtful enough to lodge Kaiti, a Greek kitty only ten weeks old (the minimum age for acceptance) in the chalet next to mine for me to comfort. We converse in Greek, of course, but are not permitted physical contact. Every morning I demand a cuddle from my personal carer, who exercises me and introduces me to three filmstar ginger and white cats fresh from filming in Italy. We are a pretty distinguished bunch one way and another. I myself am dubbed "The Comedian" because I make people laugh with my antics and sleep on my back with my legs in the air. Life has its compensations. All the same I long for freedom and to be restored to the bosom of my family.

After distributing my spare cat food to the Cats of the Rocks in Cavalaire where it is much appreciated, and placating a local lady, who tries to persuade her to adopt a Cavalaire kitten in need of a *foyer* (this means a hearth), Zanthoula telephones Wey Farm to enquire after me. The first time she rings, owing to flight delays, I have not yet arrived. The next time, Zanthoula is assured I was successfully picked up at Heathrow by a quarantine carrier, travelled well and have already been examined by a Vet and revaccinated (a statutory MAAF obligation). I was presently making friends and eating my head off, they told her. This dispels Zanthoula's apprehension, especially the last bit, which serves to confirm they had the right cat.

In the circumstances I could hardly be more comfortable The food is excellent, my carers are dedicated and Zanthoula sends me postcards, which they pin on my wall. The one I liked best has the words *"Qui vit en paix avec lui même se sent chez lui n'importe ou"* ("He who is at peace with himself is at home anywhere") under the picture of a black and white kitten.

After the regulation two weeks' isolation ordered by MAFF, my Pets are encouraged to visit me when they arrive back in England. (By this time a Christmas tree twinkles outside my French window.) I am ecstatic to see them again. The only sad thing is that, although desperate to return to my family, I cannot leave Wey Farm until my time is up. I demonstrate my desire to do so by performing a series of the back somersaults off the Captain's knee that he taught to perform me as a kitten when I want something badly.

When my Pets return to France to prepare to sail home, Zanthoula tells me she has discovered the truth of Mark Twain: "A home without a cat, and a well fed, well petted and properly revered cat, may be a perfect home, but how can it prove itself?"

26th May is significant for two reasons: it is the date of my due release from quarantine. It is also, as it happens, the date of the launch of a new Royal Yacht, *Blue Doublet*, Princess Anne's Rustler 36.

My Pets reach English shores via an overnight sail from Cherbourg (thinking, no doubt, how they miss my watch-keeping when crossing – at the regulation right angle of course – the busy shipping lanes of the English Channel). No matter, they make it, choosing Littlehampton on the River Arun as port of entry.

As my Pets wait outside Littlehampton for the tide to fill beyond the estuarial sand-bar, a steel blue abstraction of speed and power, a king of dolphins, forecast of the fine summer to come, I am told, soars into the air right in front of *Cappelle*'s bows. It hangs there for a moment, just as it did on the shield of Odysseus, bringing our Aegean odyssey to a close and blessings for new beginnings – though not before Zanthoula says, "Let's go back and do it all again!"

TWENTY-EIGHT

Riverbanking

In which I graduate as a Riverbanker.

I go to London.

When life in Littlehampton palls we sail for Dover.

At Wey Farm I am sad to say goodbye to my personal carer, whose darling I have become and to the chef in the Cats' Kitchen, who cooks my favourites. All the same I am noticeably keen to have my collar put back on and start life anew as a Ship's Cat.

On reaching Littlehampton, the Captain carries me down a ladder to *Cappelle's* riverside berth. I am so excited to be back on my own deck that I run about chirruping. On board all is as I remember.

However, on looking around I am appalled. We have evidently set up home in a distressed area. What is to happen now? Don't we have any pennies left? So much for the River Arun running through what Hilaire Belloc called a "valley of sacred water". I have never witnessed such devastation. The far bank is lined with derelict buildings. Fronting them, the twisted jib of an abandoned crane juts skywards. Apathy and defeat fog the air. Everything is broken and neglected. This is explained when we find that the river had lain directly in the path of the Frankenstorm winds of October 1987. Funnelling down the river valley, the hurricane force winds swept all before them, including pontoons, some, sadly, with boats attached.

That night I leave *Cappelle* only briefly before returning to snuggle under the familiar duvet. Next day the Captain gives me practical training in descending the ladder. I am amazed to see the river water rising and falling. At low tide *Cappelle* is enclosed by valley walls, but at full tide she rises so high I can see right across the water meadows. Although the ladder to our pontoon is extremely long when the tide is out, I soon master the art of descending backwards, paw after paw, faster and faster, until I can turn around three rungs from the bottom and jump onto the bouncing pontoon. When the weather is wet, I yowl from the bank above to be fetched. **"MEE-DOW-OW-OW-OWN,"** I plead because I am squeamish about muddy paws. If the worst happens, I sit in the cockpit sucking the mud off my toes. Flooded water meadows confine me to barracks.

This lifestyle is new. I am gaining experience. Not only am I a Ship's Cat, but I am learning to qualify as a Riparian (or Riverbanker) and must take control of my new situation. One day a lady, who introduces herself as President of the local Cats' Protection League, asks Zanthoula if that large black and white tomcat "who thinks a lot of himself" (!!) is hers! How rude! She tells Zanthoula I have set myself up as local cock-of-the-walk and that the indigenous Riverbankers tremble at my name. I am "a wrecker ball of a cat" she says. (Most satisfactory. What music to the ears.) Another time a startled dog-walker confesses to Zanthoula he had been astonished to witness me seeing off both his pooches at once (a King Charles spaniel and a whippet) leaving them with "a lot to think about", as he puts it. "Never seen anything like it!" he says. "Swelled up like a bull-frog, your cat did!"

I do confess, however, to an embarrassing occasion. On entering the cabin one day I freaked out at the sight of the Captain's brown canvas tool-roll lying on the floor. It gives me a bad fright because of an unpleasant experience that I recently suffered. (Even the memory of it gives me the collywobbles.) My Pets learn that some monster water rats have taken to making their burrows in the river bank. Out and about as usual on my nocturnal ramblings, I poke my nose into one such burrow (all in the spirit of enquiry, you understand) only to discover it to be someone's front hall. I get a very nasty rebuff from the householder, a bad-tempered, red-eyed, bewhiskered apparition, just the size and shape of the Captain's tool roll, with yellow fangs to boot. This confrontation is a lesson to me to be more circumspect in future. Crows and starlings also resent my presence. Some days they pursue me across the water meadows forcing me to crawl flat in avoidance of aerial bombardment.

Mute swans regularly come to *Cappelle* to cadge food. Six cygnets, anxious for a handout, tap on the hull. Hissing and flapping his wings, the cob takes exception to my presence. Wisely, I keep my dignity and my distance, for he possesses powerful wings and a vicious beak. Swans can behave foolishly. Two of them get themselves into big trouble one day in a rain storm. Mistaking the streaming wet glass roof of the shopping mall opposite for the surface of the river, they attempt to land on it, sliding back down the sloping glass into the guttering and getting stuck. The fire brigade has to be called to release them.

Zanthoula, as ever, is at hand to pull sticky burrs out of my fur. I manage to stay quite still while she extracts a splinter from the tip of my nose with a needle. (Where had I been putting my nose?) Whenever the Captain drives off on some errand or other I am quick to reinstate our old game of cabin tag. I also loiter outside the boatyard offices to catch a glimpse of a sassy little tortoiseshell with sunshiny eyes who lives under the wood pile. "Do you come here often?" I enquire politely, having picked up Royal manners at Wey Farm. Her scabby-looking partner, who makes his home under some railway sleepers, does not approve of me. But it is not long before I see him off. Little Miss Sunshine prefers the attentions of the good-looking mariner from foreign parts.

On an epistolary level, Lynn Truss's cat becomes a pen friend. When an article by her appears in *The Times,* I write back, introducing myself, incorporating the odd Greek tag and extolling the life of a sea-rover. Signing herself "The Cat", Lynn's cat returns the compliment on *Times* headed notepaper. While apologising for not being familiar with Greek, she admires my spirit of adventure, she says, while confessing to being of a nervous disposition herself. After once frightening herself nearly to death crossing the road, she has made up her mind never to venture so far from home again.

Leaving me in charge on *Cappelle*, my Pets do an exchange weekend with Mel and Steve for the flat in Kensington. We have an exciting time. Gale force winds blow up and the highest tide of the year closes the road bridge across the Arun. When the electricity fails, *Cappelle*'s mains plug is discovered deep under water, so Steve is kept much occupied with restoring power. (I sleep with my paws round Mel's neck to keep her company.) Mel and Steve buy t-bone steak for supper, as well as prawns from the fish market, and declare they have really enjoyed their weekend as Riverbankers. (I did my best to play host.) As well as presenting *Cappelle* with a set of Wacky look-alike table mats with matching tea-cosy as a farewell present, they tie a smart red bow round our lampshade and spread a glorious infestation of foil-covered chocolate ladybirds and fish biscuits across our pillows.

After the success of the away-weekend, Mel chooses to celebrate her birthday aboard *Cappelle*. We dress her overall with flags and gorge strawberries and cream and birthday cake in the cockpit, while across the river the Town Band plays "Sussex by the Sea". Passengers on passing boats, seeing the flags and HAPPY BIRTHDAY banner, wave and call out birthday greetings. It is a good day!

When we pay a return visit to Kensington, I sprawl on the Turkish carpet my Pets sent back from Istanbul and listen to the strident cries of the peacocks in Holland Park. For exercise I bat a ping-pong ball across the parquet floor – not a popular move in the early hours – but what else can I do to keep fit?

One thing I never bargain for, is Kurtie, Mel's shy little tabby cat, the flat's sitting tenant. Neither has Kurtie, I am sure, reckoned on her personal space being invaded by a black-and-white blunderbuss. In fact she nearly has a heart attack. Seeking immediate refuge on the top of the kitchen cupboard, she spends the duration of my visit pressed flat in the tight space between the cupboard roof and the ceiling. Nothing will persuade her to come down until she has personally witnessed bolts being shot to keep me out of the kitchen. I admit to getting bored in Kensington and, since my Pet Voyageur has been left in the hall, take to spending a lot of time sitting inside it waiting to be taken home. I am relieved when my Pets' travel bags reappear. (I am sure that Kurtie is thankful to see the back of me too.)

On a quick visit to Littlehampton to check on *Cappelle,* the Captain reports her broken into, though not seriously, "by kids" (two boys and a fat girl had been spotted). They got into the cockpit lockers, stole our hose and left the tap on, but that is all. More importantly, first to attract our attention on re-entering the yard, is a poster for the *Evening Argos* announcing: "Local Boatyard Goes Broke". The marina office is padlocked and all the staff have been dismissed, including the old foreman, a friend of mine, who has worked at the yard all his life and his father before him. In its day the yard had been quite famous. Arthur Ransome's *Lottie Blossom* was built there. The author of *Swallows and Amazons* also chose it as *Lottie Blossom's* final resting place after his last sail from France on the approach of his seventieth birthday. Round and tubby, she has no appeal for me, unlike the good ship *Cappelle* designed as a North Sea racer.

The situation at the yard deteriorates. Theft is rife, parked cars are burgled and a boat stored under cover on the hard is set on fire. Ginny, a friend of Zanthoula, living on her parents' boat parked behind it, was asleep one night when the fire breaks out. Fortunately, with a wet towel round her head, she manages to escape to telephone the police. The fire service puts the blaze out, citing arson, probably on the part of some disaffected employee. It is Ginny who shouts to us as we drive in from London, "This place is dangerous! You'd best get out of here!" We do not hesitate.

Other aspects of our situation disturb us too, in particular a drunken neighbour, whom my Pets knew as "Eddie", since he was about as qualified as a yacht skipper as was the original Eddie the Eagle as a ski-jumper. His boat stinks like a brewery. I groan out loud when I hear him stagger back from the pub. Zanthoula also has a nightmare about a prison break-out leading to some inmate attempting to abscond on a conveniently moored boat such as ours. It is something her mind is inclined to dwell on in the unhoneyed reaches of the night, especially when we are alone.

We are finalising our departure plan, when Eddie leaps ashore early one Sunday morning announcing to the world he is "leaving". With this, giving us no time to disconnect the electricity cable, he unhitches his boat and crashes his way out, forcing *Cappelle's* bows up between pontoons. A policeman, who happens to be crossing the bridge, witnesses what happens and makes haste to help us re-secure. Thankfully there is no damage other than scratched paint. (By this time Eddie and his floating brewery have careered away on the fast-flowing tide.)

When, with the weather set fair for the next forty-eight hours, we set off at 05.30 am on Guy Fawkes Day, it is a mild and misty November morning. My last sight of the River Arun is of a bottle-bank of cormorants standing sentinel on the pier. Port, starboard or straight ahead? My earnest desire is to sail straight ahead, for there lies France. But it is not to be. When "Captain My Captain" calls "Port, it is!" I, of course, reply, "Aye, Aye, Sir!"

Pottering on past Shoreham Power Station we see little movement in Brighton Marina. Beyond Newhaven and Seaford Head comes Cuckmere Haven, with its sandy beach and guddling pools, a smugglers' haunt once considered by the Germans as a strategic landing site for the invasion of Britain. Beyond Cuckmere, the chalk cliffs of the Seven Sisters, glistering in pale sunshine, undulate. It is a thrill to nudge so close to the red and white striped barber's pole of the iconic Beachy Head lighthouse. Weirder than Beachy Head is the Royal Sovereign, which appears abeam. Marking a shoal at sea, it rises from empty water on a single column like a giant bird table. Dungeness offers a bleak landmark in the fading light as we sail east along the south coast, the sea to ourselves.

At 21.35 hrs we encounter our first problem when, despite the moon shining brightly, a dense pall of cotton-wool mist descends, a phenomenon to be expected at the close of a mild November day. We hoist the radar reflector and Eagle Eyes (me) is instructed to keep watch by peering into the fluffy white blanket. On a clear day the White Cliffs are easily visible from Cap Griz Nez in France but, only yards away now, the coast of England is obscured. Suddenly I become aware of a patch of diffused light to port, which quickly transforms itself into a coaster steaming dangerously close. I let out a warning, **"W-A-A-T- C-H O-W-O-W-T!** which has Zanthoula grabbing the torch to rake our sails with its beam. At what seems like a hundred metres (and a hundred years) the coaster passes on, giving three warning blasts from its foghorn. We reckon it must be out of Folkestone.

It is high time to call Dover coastguard, who logs *Cappelle*, though fails to locate her on radar, despite our reflector. They will be guiding us in, they say, seemingly glad of something interesting to do, there being no other small sailing vessel out and about on this November night. We are to keep our radio on dual control. When we believe ourselves to be on the approximate line of approach to the harbour – though can still see nothing through the fog, we turn to port. Our approach, soon confirmed, is spot on. Abruptly, the eastern arm of the harbour mole looms above us, the harbour lights (fixed white and fixed triple red) on its end. In confirmation of our position, we also count the seventeen lights spaced along the rail terminal. Asked if we have encountered a coaster, we realise the vessel out of Folkestone had reported us. Dover is awaiting our call. A pilot launch is despatched to guide us onto a waiting pontoon. At midnight we tie up safe and sound in Dover harbour. After a good meal out of the pressure pot we turn in.

At 07.00 hrs next morning we were ready for the off. But fog lingers. Departure at 10.00 hrs is right for the tide, but at that time Channel 80 is still reporting heavy mist, though with visibility improving. Soon the Port Authorities give us permission to leave, but tell us to check with them again in the outer harbour for final clearance. There is nothing to pay.

TWENTY-NINE

We Sail the South Coast

In which we sail the glorious Goodwins.

We enter the Thames estuary.

We tie up in Gillingham Marina.

Ferries and hovercraft surround *Cappelle* as we pass St Margaret's Bay. I am on watch. The sea chatters cheerfully when we alter course for the Thames Estuary. There follows a stupendous sail. *Cappelle,* speeded by a flood tide, queens it as she weaves her way through the Goodwin Sands. We revel in the sunlit waters all to ourselves. The breeze is fresh, the micro-tipped wavelets reflect the bluest of skies – just the perfect day for a winter sail. It is times like these which tell me mine is the best profession in the world.

In days gone by the Goodwins, a ten-mile long sandbank in the English Channel, went by the name of The Shyppe Swallower. More than 2,000 ships, it is said, foundered here. There remains speculation as to the "inestimable stores and unvalued jewels" that lie "all scattered on the bottom of the sea". Is that an emerald gleam down there? Or just the glint of a cat's eye? But, if treasure does surface one day, it will be after a great storm, not in the serene weather we enjoy.

Paying due heed to lightships and buoyage, at 12.20 hrs we hoist the cruising chute to add speed and another blue to the azure of the sky and the resin blue of the sea. By 14.35 hrs we are abeam the chalk headland of the North Foreland. Here some sort of beacon has always shone by night for the safety of shipping. By the end of the seventeenth century a good fire of coals was kept burning for the assistance of sailors in an iron grate on top of flint structures on both the North and South Forelands.

As the Captain and I seek out the buoyage up the Thames estuary, a spectacular sunset scalds our sails and dyes the sea crimson. Then, under a blood red sky, we struggle to pull the cruising chute on board before the current draws us into the river. The buoys and obstacles in the traffic ahead are confusing to all eyes but mine. At 19.45 hrs, after passing the Isle of Sheppey, the Captain identifies the fortress of Sheerness, built to defend the River Medway. Above us, angry sky caverns straight from Norse mythology burrow deep into the heavens, while wild reefs of monticular cloud bank the vermilion skies as we turn into the Medway to moor outside the lock gates of Gillingham Marina.

Next morning the Captain seeks permission for *Cappelle* to enter the locking system. After the fiery crescendo of the sunset of the night before the new day dawns dull as ditchwater. But in the marina the previous evening is still the talking point, the most spectacular sunset anyone can remember.

I do, of course, lose no time in hopping ashore. With mature trees and herringbone walkways, the marina impresses. Our luck has changed! We have gone up in the world! Round-the-clock monitoring and security have failed to deter the local wildlife from enjoying its freedom and a cat may do as he pleases. Mallards waddle and cormorants hang their wings out to dry on the pontoons. I become so well-acquainted with a nonchalant urban fox, who trots along the pavement as if he owns the place, we are soon exchanging passing nods. In contrast, one look at the depressed area beyond the gasworks outside the marina gates, with its population of to-be-avoided youth, is enough for me. Out there shop windows and doors are grilled and padlocked. The front door of one unkempt dwelling has a "BUGGER OFF" notice nailed savagely across it. In case this should include me, I beat a hasty retreat back to *Cappelle*.

After Zanthoula has whooped about emptying the chandlery of all the sale-price sailing apparel from Quimper in France she takes a fancy to, my Pets get down to packing. Then, with the waterline washed and *Cappelle* safely locked into the yacht basin, we leave for the Cotswolds.

THIRTY

An English Christmas

Christmas in the Cotswolds.
In which I experience rural living.
I suffer a squirrel attack.

The first thing I notice about the pretty lodge we are to occupy is that it has a cat flap in the backdoor. To my indignation, I am not allowed out that first night, so sulk on the bow windowsill in the sitting room staring out at the surrounding park, my disapproving back to my Pets. The rustic nights, their air filled with strange blood-curdling sounds, are scary: the scuffling of badgers, the squeal of small prey, the screams of a vixen calling a dog fox and the screech of barn owls. Even the rural silence holds within it heart-stopping breathings, crepitations and hints of furtive movement in the dark. When I crawl under the duvet on the old brass bedstead, Zanthoula whispers she hopes no stranger will come knocking on the moonlit door.

In the morning the sun shines, all is light and air and I am allowed out into the walled garden. "**MIAOW, MIAOW,** come and see. Look what I've found. Why haven't we come here before? **LOOK SEE, LOOK SEE,**" I shout. The rural scene is a revelation. This is the heart of the English countryside, delightful, sensuous, with a hint of danger. If Zanthoula leaves the back door ajar, cheeky squirrels come into the kitchen to steal what they can and warm themselves at the green Aga.

I regret to say that, in my enthusiasm, I am not as circumspect as I might be. One day I enter the cat flap with extreme caution, one careful paw at a time, in the hopes of slinking under a chair unnoticed. Of course, Zanthoula does see me ...and SCREAMS. (For a moment she thinks I am another cat!) Breathing stertorously because my nostrils are blocked, not only am I plastered from head to foot in foul-smelling mud, but strung about with green duck weed to boot. Far worse than Dr Foster on his way to Gloucester, who stepped into a puddle right up to his middle, when I am chased by a lively young pointer, I mistake a weed-covered pond for a green lawn AND GO RIGHT UNDER! Alack-a-day! There is mud in my ears and mud up my nose. This is a lesson I never forget.

It is my first Christmas in England. Here we are occupying a Hansel and Gretel cottage, which cries out for seasonal decoration. My Pets lose no time in decking the halls with holly and mistletoe. A Christmas tree stands beside the fireplace. Firelight winks back from the bubble panes in the big bow window. Corsican sanctuary lights glow on the window sills, and from the ceiling hang witch balls glinting ruby red, midnight blue and emerald green.

To cap it all on Christmas Eve, in truly Dickensian fashion, the temperature plummets. Hoar frost rimes the trees in the park and the Captain builds up the fire. I protest as prickles of electricity run along my spine when Zanthoula strokes me. Outside everything snaps and crackles. Jack Frost on the roof transforms the lodge into a great big Christmas cake decoration. Above it, the scintillating lamps of throbbing stars blaze so brightly Zanthoula stretches up to touch them.

Just before midnight, when the bells of the village church begin to chime, my Pets, armed with storm lanterns, set off to crunch their way across the snowy park to midnight service. I beg them to take me with them but, most unfeelingly, they shut the front door right in my whiskers. They might have known this is a big mistake, for, keeping my wits about me, I dash through the lodge and am out via the back cat flap before you can say Christmas cracker. My Pets have just reached the church porch and are about to enter the warm glow of the interior, when I catch up with them and wrap my frost-fluffed fur round Zanthoula's ankles. Then, only momentarily taken aback by the sound of the church bells, the lights and the organ music, I stroll, nothing daunted, straight down the carpeted aisle. Behind me a crusty old verger plucks at Zanthoula's arm to hiss protestingly, "We don't allow cats in church." I well know that God Himself would welcome my entrance (after all he has laid out a red carpet), there being a Christmas moratorium for cats, who only want to sit under the pulpit and be nice to mice. A sympathetic parishioner, embarrassed by the verger's cantankerous rebuke, clutches Zanthoula's arm to whisper in her ear, "Take no notice, dear! Your cat's a lucky sign!"

All the same, Zanthoula feels obliged to scoop me up, when what she really wants is to educate the verger about the Madonna della Gattaiola, the Virgin of the Cat Flap in Italy. And to recite to him U A Fanthorpe's poem "The Cat in the Manger" about "Matthew, Mark and Luke and John / who got it wrong" for leaving the cat "an obvious and able / occupant of any stable" out of the Christmas story. Everybody knows that, with his glorious purr, the "harmless, necessary cat" lent comfort to the Holy Three at the Nativity, snuggling down between them after the cold coming they had of it.

Steve and Mel joined us. Before going to bed that night we hang our Christmas stockings on the knobs on the end of the big brass bedstead. Steve takes his breakfast in bed on Christmas morning, munching his way through the edible contents of his stocking, while the rest of us enjoy a fry-up downstairs. Outside, snowflakes duvet the park, giving us every excuse to hole up, throw more logs on the fire, roast chestnuts, feast on turkey, roast potatoes, sausages, stuffing, Stilton and mince pies, drink mulled wine, sip port, toast marshmallows, gorge ourselves on Christmas cake and chocolate log, revel in a truly storybook Christmas and, if you are me, curl up on the rag rug in front of the fire.

It is a hard winter, but at last the frost flowers fade from the windows, while the snow in the park gives way to daffodils so tall I hide in their yellow islands. Sometimes I get into trouble for returning from woodland forays trailing the stink of wild garlic. We explore Cricketty Valley with its friendly riding horses, meandering stream, cowslips and lady smocks all silver white. I meet a nice lady there called Jilly Cooper walking her dogs. (The threatening-looking Travellers we encounter, though, are not pleasant. Our district is on red alert since a posse of them has forced their rust-corroded buses and caravans onto a neighbouring farmer's field without by-your-leave. Ejection is proving problematic. We make sure the park gates are chained overnight.)

In the garden one warm afternoon, I get the impression a flying saucer is coming in to land – or at least the Royal helicopter. Then I look up to see a strange apparition. A wavering skein of black flying somethings emitting an ear-splitting buzz is weaving its way at speed towards our roof. Turning itself into a whirling tornado, the skein heads straight down our chimney. We have been invaded by a swarm of bees. They proceed to make themselves at home in our spare room, which my Pets promptly shut and bar. The swarm may be worth a silver spoon, but no bee-keeper shows any interest in collecting it. ("Go up on your roof? Not likely. What about my insurance?") Eventually, a company is found with a bee vacuum prepared to relocate the squatters.

I am never far from trouble in the Cotswolds. One day Zanthoula discovers me sick and dishevelled with a nasty bite on my head and several serious bites on my front. Despite her ministrations, within twenty-four hours I am in a bad way, moaning with pain and refusing to eat. I am rushed to the royal vet in Stroud, who had treated Princess Michael of Kent's Siamese cat when it was attacked, it was suggested, by grey squirrels. Twenty-three of my bites develop into abscesses and I am put on a course of antibiotics. The vet points out that all the deeply penetrating wounds are on the front of my body, which means I was at bay when so cruelly set upon (as I know only too well). He also comments that the perpetrators must have had "very dirty teeth". This is not what a Ship's Cat expects of life. Rough seas maybe but not an attack from a gang of death-dealing arboreal rats.

After a further course of antibiotics I am myself again. Back on form, however, trust me to land in another spot of bother. This time curiosity incarcerates the cat. I click out of the cat flap as usual one morning. It does not surprise my Pets when I stay out all day, but concerns them when I fail to return at night. Have I gone walkabout? They call and call to no avail. Next day Zanthoula goes off to see Jilly Cooper in case I might have gone visiting. Much sympathy is expressed, but no one in her household has seen me.

An interesting feature of the Big House, whose lodge we occupy, is an eighteenth-century cockpit-cum-doocot, a strikingly pretty octagonal building on two floors. The cockpit on the ground floor has been adopted as an implement store. The gardener is in the habit of unlocking and re-locking the doors, as and when he requires his gardening tools or the lawn-mower. Finding the doors wide open that morning and tempted by the intriguing whiff of pigeon and mice, I venture inside to have a look around. Then (horrors) the gardener reappears to put away his lawn-mower and I hide in alarm. The slamming of the doors that follows finds me a prisoner, with no one aware of my presence and no means of escape. It is a terrible retribution for trespassing. I keep shouting, **"MEE OWT!, MEE OWT!"** very loud, but no one hears, obliging me to remain there from Tuesday morning until Thursday evening, when the doors are re-opened by the gardener. Zanthoula is overjoyed to hear the clatter of the cat flap. Had My Pets paid the ransom, I ask? It must have been a fortune? That night, after I fill in my diary, a contented bulge purrs under the duvet. Sometimes I groan, half-stirring in my sleep, to awake with a start from a bad dream of killer pigeons and sniggering mice to find myself safe and sound again.

We continue to keep an eye on *Cappelle* in Gillingham until it is time to move on board. When the Captain carries out maintenance to the weather vane, he appropriates (rather meanly, I must say) our short-wave radio to take with him to the top of the mast to listen to Test Match Special while he works. This prompts Zanthoula to suggest that she and I send a joint postcard to the Test Match Special team protesting about being denied our favourite programme – and the reason for it. A hand-written reply addressed to "The Cabin Boy and Ship's Cat" is duly received from the programme director, Peter Baxter, offering his commiserations. He considered it bad form of the Captain to have sneaked off with the radio, and is only sorry our postcard arrived too late to be read on air.

A visit to the Tailor of Gloucester's House nearby is a must. Here sly moggy Simpkin chased mice amongst the teacups on the dresser. It was kind-hearted Simpkin, who, when his master, the Tailor, became gravely ill, commissioned the mice with their dexterous little paws, to finish embroidering the exquisite waistcoat the Mayor of Gloucester had ordered for his wedding day. I wished I could meet Simpkin, chase mice in and out of teacups and wander the ginnels of Gloucester's Cathedral Close.

Talking of happy events, Mel's and Steve's wedding, had been arranged. It was not, however, to be much fun for Kurtie and me. Denied the celebrations, we were to spend the weekend with the vet in Kensington. Little Kurtie behaves impeccably, but I blot my copy book. In fact, according to the vet's assistant, I "tried to wreck the place". A wild exaggeration, I am sure. But I don't think they would have me back.

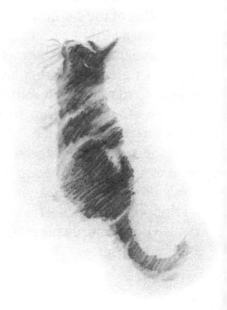

THIRTY-ONE

East Coast Interlude

In which I get to know Aldeburgh.

We survive Violent Storm Force 11.

The National Cat Club of Great Britain award me a champion rosette.

S oon afterwards, we leave for a small Suffolk town whose signature is the swish of waves on a shingle shore. In Aldeburgh I sit on the window seat of a cottage on the sea front absorbed in a book Zanthoula buys me. It is called *A Cat's Guide to England* and features Aldeburgh.

I am soon exploring Crag Path and lingering outside Aldeburgh's famous Fish & Chip shop. I am also quick to seek out the beach sheds from which the daily catch of fish is dispersed. (Some fishermen are so kind as to think I need feeding up.) The Cross Keys, formerly frequented by shanty-singing Benjamin Britten enthusiasts, also proves a good bet for a snack, while a patch of *nepeta gigantea* – to use the classic name for "cat mint" – in a certain cottage garden in the High Street is not to be missed.

On starry nights my Pets catch sight of me silhouetted against the sky on some rooftop, be it jaunty Capsize Cottage, Half Crown House (once Customs House) or Pelican Cottage, named after Sir Francis Drake's eponymous galleon built in the port of Aldeburgh in 1577, her name later changed to *The Golden Hind*.

In Aldeburgh I cannot but be aware of my affinity with the smuggling fraternity. We are all creatures of the night. In Aldeburgh's shadowy alleys I sometimes encounter the ghosts of the celebrated "Gentlemen", whose five-and-twenty ponies went trotting through the dark bearing "Brandy for the Parson / Baccy for the Clerk / Laces for a Lady / and Letters for a Spy". Slipping into doorways as the smugglers go by, I fade alongside them into just another shadow of the night.

Gales and high tides are taken seriously in Aldeburgh. In mediaeval times the Moot Hall occupied the town centre until re-sited on the seafront by the encroaching waves. The village of Slaughden, its location now taken up by the Yacht Club, similarly fell to the sea in the 1930s. When, in 1951, floods inundated the low-lying land between the River Alde and the seashore, the town (albeit temporarily) became an island. Still the restless waters ate away at the shoreline. Our own front door lies below sea-level, which makes us particularly vulnerable. Sandbags, issued by the Local Council, are stockpiled in readiness for trouble and an alert system is in place.

At the approach of the autumn equinox we awake one morning to the sounds of a gale building. With memories of the mistral, I become increasingly anxious and take to pacing the living-room floor. "What is to become of us? What if we "**CAP-SAYE-AYE-AYE-ZE?**" I miaouw, willing my Pets to pay heed. When, in desperation, I jump onto the chest of drawers and stand on my hind legs to claw at the mirror above, my urge to climb becomes plain. To placate me, Zanthoula fetches a ladder to clear the shelf over the door of ornaments. It is the highest perch in the room and I am grateful to be lifted onto it to crouch trembling as the gale rises to screaming pitch, rattling the walls. As it tears away at the fabric of the atmosphere, the wind is immense, as big as the sky, even bigger than the sea. My mind balks at it, taking refuge in blankness. Then comes the dreaded radio announcement: "Violent Storm Force Eleven imminent!" – and the air sucks back leaving a hole in it. It becomes difficult to breathe. But the anchor holds, and at last the terrifying gusts, falling short in their efforts to combine with high

I recover from the rigours of Violent Storm Force 11 in Aldeburgh.

tide and force the wild waves to overtop the sea wall, start to subside as if with fatigue.

My quiet life is not to last. I am summoned to London. My fame has spread, culminating in a flattering, not-to-be-denied, invitation to make a celebrity appearance at the National Cat Club Show at Olympia. Since, with my background of personal freedom, it is thought I might suffer from claustrophobia when incarcerated in a cage in an Exhibition Hall, I am to be provided with a double enclosure all to myself. I am to appear alongside such luminaries as "Arthur" of cat food fame. While Arthur spoons his food into his mouth with his paw happily enough, being used to a celebrity role, my own circumstances, are not so much to my liking. Even though my Pets support me with their presence throughout the proceedings, I dislike the press of strangers and am glad to get home with the rosettes with which I am awarded. These consist of a splendid National Cat Club Champion of Champions affair in red, white and blue ribbons with "To Wacky for his love of adventure from the National Cat Club of Great Britain" embossed on it in gold lettering, and a red rosette from the Norwegian Forest Cat Society, who believed I may have Norsk Skogkatt blood in my veins. (Norwegian Forest Cats, who sailed with the Vikings as mousers on their longboats a thousand years ago, are thought by some to have originated in the Aegean.) On the other hand it is good to have given pleasure to so many, who make much of me, mob my Pets for my picture and are ever eager to learn about the lives of Greek feral cats.

After Zanthoula has greeted the birth of Mel and Steve's new baby son, "Felix" – his name a compliment to my species – we continue on our way north with *Cappelle*.

THIRTY-TWO

West Coast of Scotland

In which we set up berth in Argyll.

Cappelle is damaged by a charter yacht.

In St Andrews I am appointed gang leader.

Sadly, *Cappelle* cannot be berthed in our home port of St Andrews on Scotland's east coast, for the harbour dries out. In a search, therefore, for Robert Louis Stevenson's

"Green days in forests and blue days at sea"

we seek a berth on Scotland's west coast, another of the world's most beautiful cruising grounds. My Pets inspect several marinas to find the most suitable, my own welfare being a consideration.

While exploring the coast near Oban by car one glorious day in early summer, boats bobbing on the blue water nearby, we set up a lochside picnic. Zanthoula, Katie Moragging about in the meadow, skipped along fussing over where to lay the picnic rug without squashing too many flowers. This does not just mean buttercups and daisies, but a high-value assortment of lady-smocks, cat's eye speedwell, ragged robin, scarlet pimpernel, Scots bluebell, red and white clover, birdsfoot trefoil, butterfly orchids, heart's ease pansies, purple-tufted vetch, stitchwort and goodness know what all. In the peat bog, kingcups, cotton grass and yellow flag iris flourish.

When replete with picnic fodder, we lay back chewing blades of grass. Zanthoula made daisy chains, and I have a satisfying scratch 'n roll session before chasing field mice. After she has folded the picnic rug, Zanthoula goes back to straighten the flowers we sat on. (She is silly like that.)

Of one mind, we know without a doubt that this will be our next paradise.

We therefore lose no time in taking a berth at nearby Ardfern. Built on Loch Craignish around a pier once used by Clyde Puffers to service local freight, Ardfern marina forms part of a traditional west coast village. Although I shall be obliged to share the pontoon with all comers (including, as it turns out, Royalty – more of this later), the site has immediate appeal as "good cat country" since it affords me direct access to over the hills and faraway for a spot of Hey Nonny Yes-es! (after all I am a tomcat) until the biscuits in my blue bowl call me home. The views are sensational. In the distance rear the Paps of Jura: the Mountain of Gold, the Holy Mountain and the Mountain of the Kyle. Fulfilling the platonic vision of mountains, now lost in mist, now etched so clearly against the western sky we know rain is on its way, they point their perfect cones to the heavens.

In rough weather at high tide, even at a distance, we detect the rumble of the Corryvrechan whirlpool. I shudder as my ears pick up its ominous roar. The maelstrom is to be experienced to be believed, they say – should you survive. Situated between the islands of Jura and Scarba, it enjoys the reputation of being one of only three places in the world once marked on the Admiralty Chart as "unnavigable".

On the far side of Loch Craignish straggles Eilean Righ, the Royal Island, named, some believe, for King Olav of Norway, who died nearby. Here lies a primitive petroglyph such as I remember from Greece, in this case a cup mark pecked into a rock, evidence I am once again in ancient lands. The blue heartlands draw me. Maybe we should seek the perfect island, an amalgam of the best features of all those we know.

Ardfern is so sheltered it is a "white" area, which mobile phone signals do not penetrate. Some yachtsmen, seeking peace, welcome this. (Some bewail the lack of communication.) Other inviting aspects of Ardfern are that theft is unheard of (a record soon to be broken) and that *Cappelle* can over-winter in the water. While my Pets tuck her into her berth I parade the pontoon to familiarise myself with my new surroundings.

Blocking entry to the Sound of Jura is the formidable Dorus Mhor (the Big Gate), where tides meet and the incoming sea sweeps up the Sound to a dead end in Loch Craignish, the volume of water being forced out towards the Firth of Lorn. Little experience of tides after sailing the Aegean, means we face a learning curve.

However, it is too early to prep for adventure for Fate has other ideas. The Captain is studying tide tables and considering our cruising options when, with strong cross-winds blowing, *S/Y Triskelion,* a bareboat charter yacht with an inexperienced crew, miscalculating wildly, attempts to leave the berth beside us at speed. Slicing along our port side, its anchor fluke gauges out three of our stanchions. With a damaged hull and no port guardrail, the Captain is not prepared to start cruising. The argument between the insurers and perpetrators, and the subsequent repairs, mean exploring has to take second place.

The delay gives us breathing space to install GPS, birth child of the Gulf War, a modified version of which was demonstrated to us in Tinos by yachtsman, Leo, father of a serving officer. I do well to remember that SatNav is an adjunct. It gives you a position on earth (or above the earth, if you get it wrong) but fails to tell you about tides and tide races, or give warning if a concealed rock lies in your path. The prudent sailor keeps his tried and true navigational aids, and, of course, his Ship's Cat, as back-up – and knows how to employ them. Technocats, like me, understand this.

Meanwhile Zanthoula forages for blackberries while I wander on the wild side, or stravaig as they say. One yachting family, who admire my prowess at catching my own tea, brings me a splendid fish. When they drop it glistening on the pontoon in front of me, to their delight it proves too tempting and I pounce and swallow it whole, head to toe. That night it lies heavy within and causes an internal upheaval that has me rushing outside in the night to retch it up, still in one piece. Greed got the better of me. "Think on't, Wackster!"

Once I stay out a whole day and night on the look out for the White Lady of Craignish, who is said to haunt the area, though all I see are pale whorls of mist. Zanthoula visits me for a chat from time to time. But I never go home. When at last I do so, I curl up and sleep for nearly as long as I have been away, awaking refreshed and satisfied that I know my territory.

My life becomes one of strenuous leisure, as suits to my kind. Sometimes we return to Fife where I practise the indolence necessary to feline well-being in an Aga-warm kitchen and on sprawly beds. Our railed garden, facing onto a town street, is a substitute for the deck I am used to commanding. I patrol its low wall, just as if I am strolling along my own cap rail, introducing myself to passers-by (should I like the look of them) and making friends. When the click of the garden gate heralds an invasion of our sovereign territory, I welcome only those who have my approval.

The Captain fixes a cat flap in the back door and I am soon circumnavigating our four-house block by means of its walls and rooftops. In the early hours the streets are quiet and it is then that I cross over to go clubbing with my dustbin cronies back o' the buildings. My land-lubbing mates are mesmerised by my tales of derring-do on the high seas. We warble to a perigee moon, sing to a small guitar, scavenge, play tag and practise the Highland Fling. I soon learn to yell, "Shut yer geggie!" and "Gie it laldie!" It is inevitable that I am voted gang leader. I am strict with my band of brothers, particularly that "heid banger", who doesn't mind his manners. When dawn lightens the sky, my classic cry of "*Extra omnes!*" papal style, has them dispersing double-quick to their respective cat flaps. Of course, I would appreciate a "bidey-in", as they say, or live-in girlfriend. (There is a popsy named Peigi near the Pancake Place who truly pickles my walnuts.) But then sailors have a wife in every port. Being of similar opinion to James Hogg, the Ettrick Shepherd, who wrote:

"O, love, love, love!
Love is like a dizzyness
It winna let a puir body
Go about his bisiness "

I consider it wise not to commit myself.

THIRTY-THREE

A Cat of Distinction

In which I encounter Hamish McHamish,

famous son of St Andrews.

Back on the West Coast I socialise with celebrities, including
Royalty.

One night, as we are practising the Reel of the 51st (a very popular
dance) back o' the buildings, a stranger strides into our midst.
Silence falls. We cats exchange glances. The last thing I want is a
rammy, the dreaded free-for-all, to spoil the ceilidh.

The newcomer is a massive ginger tom with an air of superiority.
I can see he means business. We eye one another. "Tread cautiously,
Wackster," I say to myself. Ever the diplomat and knowing myself the
interloper in the Auld Grey Toon, I recognise the newcomer's natural
authority, so bowing courteously, I wait for him to speak first. In a civil
manner he then introduces himself as Hamish McHamish, Cool Cat About
Town. He certainly has the *parlez-vous*. He tells me he has the honour
of reigning supreme hereabouts, having been granted the Freedom of
the City. The good citizens of St Andrews have even hung his portrait-
in-oils in the Town Hall, he tells me. Now he is about to be sculpted in
bronze by a famous artist.

After apologising for trespassing on his domain without first seeking
his permission, keeping my dignity I answer in kind, explaining that I

have the honour to be: "At your service, Sir, Chief Petty Officer Wacky MacWackster, Ship's Cat of Greek extraction, in the area in the pursuit of my duties." I would be spending most of my time at sea, I tell him, so there is no suggestion of my harbouring any notion of infringing on his territorial rights. Known across far-flung parts as "Wacky", I believe myself to be of the bloodline of the Wacky MacWacksters of Auchtermuchty. (This is a bit of a stretch, but plausible, since the Greeks – take, for example, the Ship's Cats of Pytheas, the Odysseus of the North – are believed to have explored as far north as Scotland.)

Accordingly, Hamish and I, each recognising the other's claim as a Cat of Distinction, become allies. He even offers to autograph his latest book for me. In return I casually make mention of the Champion of Champions rosette with gold-tooled dedication presented to me by the National Cat Club of Great Britain. On occasion I invite Hamish through my cat flap, when we spend an hour or two in front of my red Aga. He, in turn, introduces me to the brightest nightspots in town and coaches me in how to cross busy South Street by day in safety. (The trick is to wait at the foot of the traffic lights until the human beans assemble and then cross amongst them.)

Pytheas, the Odysseus of the North, was a product of wanderlust like Homer's Odysseus. Born into a Phocaean colony in Massalia (Marseilles) he had sailed north in 325 BC in search of the Kassiterides, the Tin Islands (now known as the British Isles) and lands beyond. While exploring northern shores he encountered killer whales and giant "mammal fish" (probably basking sharks). When a tribe told him of wondrous lands rich in amber further north, he set his sextant and sailed until the seas turned gelid. He wrote a book called Περί του Ωκεανού (*About the Ocean*). Pytheas may well have mentioned my part in this voyage, for I am certain I sailed with him. The memory makes my head swim and I find myself dissolving into another past life, clinging on by my toenails as I stand duty on the pointy prow of Pytheas's high-sided long boat while the northern waters turned to ice.

My desire to be sailing full and bye playing chess with the rick-rack

In St Andrews I casually make mention of the Champion of Champions rosette awarded me by the National Cat Club of Great Britain.

waves, has to be curtailed for reasons I explained. But confinement to the marina has its compensations, for I am amazed to find myself tripping over celebrities. (They, of course, would say they were tripping over me, but this is not true, for I am adept at the side-step.) My first encounter is with an elfin-faced young woman with white marble skin, wide-apart eyes, go-to-bed hair and high Icelandic cheek bones. The most noticeable thing about her is that she is dressed in grunge, which looks strangely out of place in a West Highland village. She lets the tattered edge of her black satin evening skirt trail in the mud and the pointed sleeves of her lace shift hang over her hands. She and her boyfriend relish the home-cooking in the Ardfern Craft Centre, which incidentally serves my favourite scallops (not to mention the sticky toffee pudding my Pets enjoy).

This fey young lady is on a mission to buy an island, she tells me, Eilean Righ the one presently in mind. Ever since she was a little girl, she says, she has dreamed of having her very own island with resident Highland Piper. It sounds so romantic! When the couple are asked how they would earn a living, she says, "Music." Her name is Björk. Her singing voice, shivery and other worldly, is as wild as the hills. She also knows just how to stroke a cat with her long, combing fingers. (Was she thinking of me when she brought out her video, "I should buy a boat cat"?)

Despite my initial shock of recognition over the next celebrity I encounter, I manage to keep my cool and sketch a half-bow, before losing my sang-froid completely to leap aboard the nearest boat to get out of her way. *Blue Doublet*, a Rustler 36, has drawn in, its skipper pausing to pass the time of day with the Captain, while indicating to his busy companion to follow suit. (The Captain goes quite pink at this, I notice.) Just beforehand I had come head-on with a sporty female bean striding down the pontoon shouldering a duffle bag. Long-legged and agile, she looks most seaworthy in her navy blue Breton cap. I suspect she has a head for heights, for she is a well-known pharologist. Being Greek, I know what that word means, since it derives from the original lighthouse, the giant "Pharos" of Alexandria. The lady in question, who is patron of the Northern Lighthouse Board, collects lighthouses and is known to have visited as many as eighty of those strung out along the 6,000 miles of Scottish coastline, often in her own boat *Blue Doublet*. What makes my heart miss a beat is that, as well as being a pharologist, she is also The Princess Royal, and here am I sharing our pontoon with her!

At Ardfern we are protective of our Princess, just as she is protective of the lighthouses. (Lately she has supported the remarkable Skerryvore, pride of the Hebrides, against extensive wind farming.) We keep our lips sealed about her presence amongst us. I even stay buttoned up when consorting with the local moggies, full of craic and blether as they are. A hint of a snooper in the boat yard and we spread disinformation. Known affectionately as "the love birds" the couple support the local supermarket when they stock up for the boat. And of course we live-aboards hug it to ourselves when HRH spends her birthday amongst us, while the BBC is solemnly reporting her to be at Balmoral.

"I've got the world on a string!" I sing to myself, wondering where that string will pull me next.

THIRTY-FOUR

The Corryvrechan

*In which it is my privilege to skipper **Cappelle**
through the notorious Corryvrechan Whirlpool.*

I am not long in finding out. All the while the terrifying, but seductive,
roar of the Corryvrechan, the "Whirlpool of the Speckled Plaid" and
the distant howling of the Grey Dogs in the Little Corryvrechan,
assails our ears. There is a Pictish belief in the Corryvrechan as the holy
grail, the womb of creation. It is sometimes called the Scottish Scylla
and Charybdis. Not many sailors are acquainted, as I am, with Homer's
original.

A myth links the Pass of the Grey Dogs with Cailleach Bheur, the Old
Hag of Winter, who is said to wash her plaid in its waters as the year
draws to a close, scrubbing it for three days until the coverlet is dazzling
white, when she draws it out to spread across the land in a blanket of
snow. They say that when the waves rise in a tottering tower, those close
enough to the Cailleach in their dying moments see her tie her kerchief
over her white hair.

A Viking prince called Breachan once courted the daughter of a Lord of
the Isles. Not wishing her to marry a foreign sea rover, the proud father
challenged Prince Breachan to prove his worth by anchoring his vessel
for three days and nights in the Corryvrechan. To this end Breachan
was advised to prepare three cables, one woven from the wool of a West

Highland horned sheep, one fashioned from hemp and the third from the plaited hair of local virgins. The first night the cable of sheep's wool broke, the second night the hemp cable snapped. The cable made of virgins' tresses survived until just before dawn on the third night, when it too parted, with the loss of the Prince and his boat. (The tale suggests that the final cable failed because one of the maidens was not as pure as she was cracked up to be.)

Having survived the original Scylla and Charybdis, I make up my mind to accept the challenge the Corryvrechan offers. I know I must keep my wits about me when undertaking the responsibilities of Ship's Cat on such an enterprise. Despite my well-developed sea legs, I have to submit to the uncomfortable safety harness, with lifeline attached, which the Captain insists on – otherwise I am threatened with the ignominy of being shut in the forepeak throughout the glorious adventure. For my part I sharpen my claws – the sharper the better for attaching oneself in extremity. Zanthoula and I will communicate on how to act. (One thing we both know without a doubt is that we enjoy mutual understanding in such a way as to go in and out of each other's minds without effort.)

First and foremost is the choice of wind and weather. After the Captain has committed the tide tables to memory, nothing stands in our way and, on a perfect Odyssean morning, the sun sparkling on a calm blue sea, the tide slack, we stand off Dorus Mhor awaiting the westbound flood to carry us into the Corryvrechan.

Though porpoises gambol, an eerie atmosphere develops as we approach the whirlpool's entrance. A tide line is drawn across the water. Why do I feel *Cappelle* is trespassing? When we enter the gulf it feels alien, as though, iron-bound on both sides by rocks about which I have reason to be watchful, these menacing waters rightly belong to wildness and myth, rather than to an insignificant wooden sloop under the command of a Ship's Cat venturing in out of curiosity and bravado. "Abandon hope, all ye who enter here," it seems to say.

The sea, dotted with watery question marks, indents and whorls that presage worse to come, looks unnaturally flat and brooding. Something spooky snatches at the surface from below. A liquid bulge, as sweetly smooth and shining as a waxed mushroom, slowly lifts its mesmerising bald pate beside us and then subsides, simmering. A few bubbles rise around its edge as in a boiling pot; it is as if the mound lacks the energy to lift its head just yet. Steadied by my outstretched tail, I turn, glad to have sharpened my claws, to find these uncanny upheavals repeating themselves at random around us as they gain more and more energy. But the new engine holds us semi-steady for now at least, bolstering a flimsy sense of control, as the tide, bent on enforcing dominance, strives to steer us towards a newly formed vortex. I know this has the power to pinion us like a needle on a gramophone record. If wind and weather take a turn for the worse the sinister circle could swirl into a pyramid and spout explosively as high as the mast.

It is my task, according to the chart, to keep *Cappelle* as well south of the central line of the Corryvrechan channel as possible, while avoiding the tidal stream setting up the NE side of Jura, which is intent on propelling us into the outfall that lies two tenths of a nautical mile off the SW corner of Scarba. (Here cheeky shearwaters, totally at home, show off, "Strictly" fashion, flicking and dancing across the crests of waves.)

The Corryvrechan's unique underwater topography consists of a variety of features, including a pit descending more than 200 metres below the seabed, at the bottom of which gravel swirls endlessly, self-polishing. Another feature is a basalt pinnacle rising from a depth of 70 metres to reach up to 29 metres below the surface at its rounded top. This can drive the booming Atlantic tides to 8.5 metres and waves to a height of over 30 feet. Of course, with *Cappelle,* we have chosen slack conditions, engine on, the sails to steady, the Captain's feet firmly planted as he stands at the wheel while we ride the irregular upheavals, turgid, shockingly unpredictable, this way and that, foretaste enough to fire the imagination on the subject of the passage in less benign circumstances.

When *Cappelle* pops out the far side like a triumphant little cork from a bottle, we are under no illusions. We are also under the spying eyes of the red deer on the heights of Jura. Its cliffs are fringed with antlers poking up like hat-pegs. Above us, golden eagles gyre in the thermals. As well as offering gratitude to Aphrodite Euploia (as always) for our safe passage, I give thanks to Shony, the Celtic god of the sea. (On winning the Golden Globe Round-the-World Race in 1968, Robin Knox-Johnston poured a libation to Shony over the stern of *Suhaili*.)

Then we bequeath the Corryvrechan to the porpoises, stormy petrels and Minke whales to whom it rightly belongs. In 1945 the Gulf featured as a location in Powell and Pressburger's celebrated film *I Know Where I'm Going*, footage of the Corryvrechan being effectively used in back projections in the film, with the cast in a replica boat rocking on gimbals in the foreground having buckets of water hurled over them. (I am glad I didn't take part in the film. I would have objected to buckets of water being chucked over me.)

To be honest, with a hint of mares' tails in the sky I have a yen to be back in the comfort of Ardfern before the sun, now setting in a clear sky, turns the Atlantic into a blood bath. Ardfern is where we head, timing our passage back through the Pass of the Grey Dogs for the slack again. Here Prince Breachan's faithful hound, after failing to rescue his master, met his own end that fateful day. As we come through, I detect an echo of the woeful cry of the poor wretch.

When we digest the lessons of our Corryvrechan experience, we are satisfied we took the passage at just below our capabilities, leaving something in reserve, always the best plan.

My Pets devour jeely pieces for tea – chunks of newly baked bread, thick buttered, spread with homemade bramble jelly purchased at the Post Office. Later Zanthoula serves mackerel with gooseberry jam for supper. (I prefer mine plain.) The scallops in Aphrodite shells to follow are mouth-watering. Then we settle down as anchorites again (meaning, for us, those who rest at anchor, not those who inhabit caves.)

THIRTY-FIVE

A Friendship is Cemented

In which I spend a joyous day
with a pen pal on the island of Coll.

We are discussing where to go next when, with impeccable timing, serendipity steps in. I am in receipt of a letter from a pen pal, who lives on the island of Coll. He is a literary cat I first contacted from Greece. Both being islophiles, we continue the correspondence. His Pet is a Lady Artist, who adds delightful illustrations to his letters. My letters did have a smattering of Greek in them, but they aren't a patch on Fabbydou's. He himself is a handsome ginger tom of tremendous character, who growls when he is happy. (I so look forward to hearing him growl – as I hope he will – when we meet.)

The Captain invests in an Admiralty Tidal Stream Atlas before we set sail. I must keep my nerve, for at many points along the West Coast, even in calm weather, the sea begins to swirl and bubble, a reminder of the Corryvrechan, as a million tons of water come to a dead halt before gathering momentum in a new direction. I feel this in the Dorus Mhor as we set out, engine on, along the Firth of Lorn, before bearing to port up the broad seaway that is the Sound of Mull, where we sail with a strong breeze astern, the genoa poled out and the main sail goose-winged. To port lies the social scene of Mull, to starboard the lonely reaches of mainland Morven.

It is in the Sound of Mull I chance upon my first sea monster in Scottish waters. I can't believe my eyes! The creature is too big to be real, a huge grey-brown shadow beneath the sea half as long as a London bus, its mouth open as it sucks in plankton. I notice with a shudder there is plenty of room for me inside that cavernous maw. I would hardly even class as a tidbit! But basking sharks are gentle giants, and if one swallowed me it would be by mistake. (Since the result would be the same, this is small consolation.) I am thankful we didn't bump into this particular Triton when he was asleep. It would have been like slamming into a harbour mole.

Towards the end of the northern leg of the Sound, we pass Tobermory, a gem of a village with a curve of the prettiest coloured houses I ever did see. I want to meet the Seafaring Cats of Fishnish and the Tobermory Cat, who became famous by being himself. (They say the Tobermory Cat tried to learn to be special, but it didn't work. When he relaxed, as we all should, he found he was special anyway, and everyone wanted to meet him! As for myself, I do not have to try to be special because I was BORN special.)

But tying-up in Tobermory has to wait because we are expected on Coll. I raise the antennae of my whiskers to pick up direction and soon, way across open water, there is the island, low-lying like something lunar. (We could tell that God was in a good mood when he made Coll; it has a certain something about it.) As ever, on a boat, seeing is one thing, arriving is another. But the glorious sunny weather, common for Coll, since its low profile does not generate clouds, is in our favour. Indeed its anchorages are only suitable in good conditions. I have a quick wash and brush up to calm the nerves and spruce myself to meet my host. Then, with the Captain's help, I ensure *Cappelle* is ship-shape and Bristol fashion for my meeting with Fabbydou. There must be none of the old one-two, one-two which can happen when two tomcats meet face to face. (This is unlikely, since we have both been brought up in the school of good manners.) We will hightail a greeting, as is accepted etiquette in polite feline society. I do hope Fabbydou growls. Then I can be sure he is pleased to see me.

Purposefully we negotiate the inlet which protects Coll's main settlement of Aringour ("Sheiling of the Goats"), two rows of trim white cottages with a hotel, a post office, a café and a village store, not to mention lots and lots of happy people. Putting out two anchors and fixing tyre fenders, we tuck in beneath ancient walling, a kindly Collach promising to keep an eye on things. Oh what a joyous arrival. The Lady Artist meets us with a lovely smile and Fabbydou rumbles a magnificent growl. What more could I ask? Fabbydou says it was good of me to sail so far over fathoms of the deep under a misty moon (a bit of exaggeration there). He doesn't think much of the sea himself, he says. He hasn't even enjoyed the ferry crossing from Oban, except for the renowned fish and chip supper provided by Caledonian Macbrayne.

We spend a splendid day, escorted all over the island by the Lady Artist, not just on the road north and the road south, but bumping over the sand dunes too. Everyone knows her and waves. Lunch is taken in the hotel garden (cock-a-leekie soup with added fish-stock for Fabbydou and me). I don't know what the human beans have for pud, but I expect it is roast rhubarb with Irn-Bru ice-cream – they all like that. Then we sit in the Lady Artist's garden gazing at distant Staffa and "The Dutchman's Cap", islands that look just like ships at anchor in the blue, blue sea. The human beans take their coffee with a wee dram of *uisge beatha* (whisky), but Fabbydou and I sup the nutritious tadpole water at the edge of the pond. Then we lark about and sing the skipping song, "Ye canny shove yer granny off a bus, PUSH, PUSH", as we spring up and down. Afterwards we poke our paws down rabbit holes in case any *Whisky Galore* contraband might yet remain secreted. (I know it is the wrong island, but Coll had its shipwrecks too.)

Later the Lady Artist drives us to Breachaha ("the field speckled with wild flowers") to see the ruined castle. Here she gets down to gather mushrooms. Then we rock boldly across the flower-studded coastal grassland overlying shell sand known as the machair that stabilises the dunes. Beside us, little lochans, habitat of the red-throated diver, glow with white water-lilies, while a corncrake in the grass repeats the rasping cry that imitates the buzzing of a faulty electric cable. Soon we descend the dunes into Feall Bay, a spectacular semi-circle of golden sand from which Zanthoula plucks a fan of scarlet seaweed to take home. (She is one of those pocket-full-of-pine-cones people.)

The Lady Artist tells us a tale of Feall's recent history. A fin whale (second only in size to a blue whale) was washed up in Feall Bay, which lies open to the Atlantic. The islanders were dismayed when they heard that the carcass of this rare visitor was to be confiscated by those bullies in the National Museum of Scotland, eager to study and preserve it. The law was on the side of the bullies too, since the fin whale's carcass was over twenty-five feet long, which classed it as a "Royal Fish" (even though it was a mammal) and therefore the property of the Crown, though the islanders knew it as their own.

Thus the poor fin whale was left rotting on the beach for weeks (I think I caught a whiff of it in Ardfern) before the authorities agreed on a method of removal. Hours before this was to take place, a determined bunch of Collachs, keen to erect a mandible arch above the ferry terminal as an attraction to tourists when the fuss died down, armed themselves with a chain saw and hacked off the 550lb jaw bones. Then they dragged them away by tractor and buried them beneath a sand dune. But a local youngster, bribed by a Mars bar, gave the game away when cross-questioned by a policewoman. Sadly for the islanders, the whale's jaws were soon to join the carcass they belonged to in faraway Edinburgh.

The sun is so hot Zanthoula is tempted to swim, but settles for a paddle instead. (She is glad not to have succumbed to the former temptation when we meet the sunburn sufferers.)

Our trip to the south east of Coll is followed by another to the north east to Sorisdale, a deserted crofting and fishing village, where we clamber its rocky shores and look out across the neon blue waters beyond to the Cairns of Coll and Ardnamurchan Point. Archie and Hector, now deceased, were bachelor twin brothers who had lived in Sorisdale all their lives. It was their custom to place their armchairs on opposite sides of the hearth. As time went on, pressure was put on them to accept television, but the twin whose chair faced away from the set could never be persuaded to turn it round since it had always faced the other way. On the rare occasion he wished to glance at the screen, he merely moved his head to look over his shoulder.

A thriving stud of the pearl grey Eriskay ponies, a rare breed, lives on Coll but no toads or venomous creatures, no foxes, no squirrels and NO RABBITS – so Fabbydou had never known the joy of the rabbit chase. (I think he envies me that.) Rabbits are banned; if they were to spread to the neighbouring island of Tiree and make burrows, it might sink, since Tiree is made of sand, not solid gneiss like Coll.

Fabbydou and I reminisce. He tells me the story of how he frightened the Big Boy Cousins – all five of them! When, cock-a-hoop with their own importance, they went camping near Castle McColl, Fabbydou tricked them by posing as Clan Chief Rory of the Flaming Red Beard, with Mr Mistake, his sidekick (the shy whitey with a dodgy eye he lived with) complicit as the Wee White One-Eyed Ghost. When it grew dark, the Big Boy Cousins ran whooping into the castle, no longer the haunt of warriors, deerhounds, braided servants with shiny buttons, yummy haunches of venison and maidens in pokey hats with floaty chiffon veils, but of cobwebs, flapping pigeons, bird-droppings, rats, mice, squirmy worms, slugs and beetles. It was eerie in there. It smelt bad too. "Yoo Whoo-oo. Yoo Whoo-oo. Fearties. Fearties." The Big Boy Cousins must feel their way in the scary dark along slippy-slimy-stinky walls. Then suddenly they were scrambling back down the spiral stone staircase, wailing and crying, wringing their hands and falling over each other in their haste to get out. Up there at the top of the stair Clan Chief Rory had waggled his Flaming Red Beard right at them, they sobbed. They had seen him. And the one eye of a small white ghost had glowered at them menacingly in the dark. Fabbydou sighs with pleasure at the recollection of the success of his plan and I revel in the joke with him.

I like islands for their otherness, for the sagacity of their people, not learned from books, and for their feeling for the unbroken ring of life. I have put that wonderful day on Coll into my memory box and tied it with ribbon. When Fabbydou and I raise our tails in farewell, we squeeze our eyes at one other in recognition of our affinity. The pen-pal correspondence will continue.

THIRTY-SIX

We Move Berth

In which we move to Holy Loch via the Crinan Canal.
We encounter a monster in the River Clyde.

One thing I like about the live-aboard life is the knowledge that all your comforts go with you, on a whim, anywhere, everywhere. If conditions are right – it's up anchor and off. That is all there is to it. As the dog days of summer draw to a close and the nights lengthen, the Captain resolves to move to Holy Loch, a one-time US submarine facility where we will take advantage of its temperature-controlled boat shed. It will mean *Cappelle* can be under cover for maintenance.

The most convenient route is via the Crinan Canal, a short cut across the Kintyre peninsula only nine miles long, constructed in the late eighteenth century so that shipping need no longer sail the dangerous eighty-mile passage around the Mull of Kintyre. In 1963 it served as the location for the boat chase in the Bond film *From Russia with Love*. At twelve feet, it should be deep enough, even after a dry summer, to give *Cappelle* good clearance, even adding four inches to her draught for fresh water.

Tree-sheltered, the canal curves through the countryside not far from the Great Moss. In 1847 Queen Victoria sailed it in a Royal barge pulled by horses ridden by postilions in scarlet coats. I look forward to the trip. (Even, perhaps, to playing hookey along the tow-path.) But as it turns out, I am not in sympathy with the popular song "The Crinan Canal for Me" for "From Ardrishaig to Crinan" (the other way round in our case) is far from "the best trip A've bin in". As we leave Ardfern dark-hearted clouds are gathering. Then, as if it has something to say, heavy rain comes hurrying up Loch Craignish to meet us.

The weather worsens. It is soon so bad that by the time we pass the sad remains of the old coal puffer, the *Vital Spark* to reach the wider water of Bellanoch Marina, visibility is virtually nil. After suffering a second drenching night we are glad to exit the locking system en route for the Holy Loch via the Kyles of Bute and the River Clyde.

There is a heart-stopping shock in wait for us as we proceed up stream. We are almost at the entrance to the Holy Loch, with me perched in the stern in a rare moment of leisure taking in the magnificent panoramic view "doon the watter", as they say. Suddenly I am rendered speechless. I can't even squeak as a sea monster, water streaming off its gunmetal grey back, rises silently out of the river right on our tail. When I regain my voice, I let out a strangled cry, "**WHAT THE AHHH! ...H-E-E-L-P.**" It has to be a humpbacked whale of monstrous proportions. At this Zanthoula recovers enough to grab me and we both gaze trembling at the great creature's piggy eyes and snub nose as it stares at us before slowly sinking into the deeps whence it came, the waters closing over its head. When we realise it was a nuclear submarine on its way to Gareloch I am so thankful for deliverance that I collapse all of a heap and have to be revived with cat biscuits. (We got used to seeing these monsters during our time in Holy Loch, sometimes in the form of a narrow island that appeared at the mouth of the loch before moving slowly on. But, never again, thank goodness, do we encounter the beastie at such shockingly close quarters.)

After I have stopped shaking, making use of my natural-born global positioning facility, I reckon the compass headings for Holy Loch to be 55 deg. 58.3N / 4 deg 53.8W. And so it proves. Fortunately, the entrance to Holy Loch is hazard-free – except, of course, if a submarine should surface!

What we look forward to are those tumbleweed days of messing about on boats picnicking among the porpoises in warm sunshine. Nowhere is more beautiful than Scotland when the weather gives of its best. The air is limpid, its clarity such that the mountains stand out in silhouette, the sea sparkles and porpoises swoon upwards through pressure waves to greet you with wide smiles. At the end of such a day, we would relax in the cockpit with a sundowner. (I get Dreamies – they don't give me many on account of a build up of adipose tissue. "Not with all the exercise I take," I think to myself.) The human beans, their faces sweetened in the light of evening, and I then listen to the ripple of the sea along the hull and the soft clunk of the anchor chain tweaked by an eddy. Not until the rising moon begins to etch the horizon in silverpoint and the air grows chilly is it time for us to retreat below.

But there is no way of fast-forwarding winter. *Cappelle* is due out of the water. Meanwhile spruce is obtained from Hull for a new mast, a replica of her original. (There are few wooden masts left these days and it would be a sacrilege to spoil a classic boat with a metal pole.) There are further tasks to undertake also to comply with EU strictures. With all the EU bother I am a little worried about whether I myself fall foul of regulations, but I am assured I comply. In fact 'tis my belief, as I hasten to note in this diary, that a Ship's Cat should be mandatory for all ships that aspire to the name. Certainly, the Captain could not do without me. I am his feline strong man with a side order of brains, that's me.

We do spend a few nights of winter chill on board, the sort of weather that makes sparks of electricity fly off the fur. When the temperature drops to four degrees below, Zanthoula retires to her berth wearing everything she can lay hands on, including ski socks (two pairs), thermal gloves and her woolly hat (the one with the bobble on top) pulled down over her ears. I soon join her inside her sleeping bag. This is nice for her since we cats have a higher body temperature than human beans. We are most cosy. Neither of us has any inclination to get up the following morning. When we do, it is too slippery to disembark until the sun has melted the sheet ice that glazes the deck.

THIRTY-SEVEN

Extrasensory Perception

In which I exercise second sight.
I visit the wreck of a Greek sugar ship.
I share sailing mishaps with the next generation.

Born of a goddess, I share with the Scots the gift of second sight:

"O hark, O hear! how thin and clear
The horns of Elfland faintly blowing!"

Walking the thin line between light and dark, I am aware of the spirit world. Sometimes I stand poised on its borders, never quite venturing over the line in case I can't find my way back. When we are home on the east coast and winter truly sets in, I unexpectedly encounter Snegurochka, the Ice Maiden, daughter of the Snow Queen. To my surprise she slides off our roof in a flurry of snowflakes to fall in a sparkling array at my feet. She wears diamonds in her hair and smiles at me. We play snowballs and chase. I don't dare let her pick me up because she might have fallen in love and the warmth of her feelings might have caused her to melt.

I see kelpies, malevolent water sprites in the form of horses that haunt the lochs and streams of Scotland rejoicing in drownings. Loch Eck is home to many kelpies. (I expect the Lady of Craignish rides them.) In my nightmares Artemis's broomstick sometimes turns into a kelpy. I keep away from the water's edge when I hear the whinny and snort of prancing horses, especially near waterfalls. One can never be too careful.

Selkies are interesting too. Their heads bobbing above the waves, they gaze at you with basilisk eyes. They may be seals, but some are shape-shifters too. People with second sight like me recognise which are the true seals and which are those that shed their skins and transform themselves into human bean form to become Mer People. I try to persuade Zanthoula not to swim at sunset on an ebb tide because she might be lured away by a Merman she presumes is a seal. (I am pretty sure she won't though, because, after the Aegean sea, she finds Scottish waters chilly.)

Cappelle is placed on a cradle outside the boat shed for the raising of the new mast. Launching is always fraught. It is busy work with split pins, spreaders, halyards and fuss, until at last comes the cry of "Everybody off!" (including me) as we make way for the slipway lift to lower her into the water as the tide fills. Everyone lends a hand, even those who don't belong. Passers-by pause to watch, take photographs, and join in to help (or get in the way). Someone asks Zanthoula who owns *Cappelle* and when she replies, "Me," said, "Will you marry me?" (Anyway, she says she can't, so that is all right.)

There is a problem. *Cappelle* has been out of water for several months, which is undesirable for a wooden boat. As the tide ebbs, there is an urgent need to move her into deep water. But at this point inspection reveals a leak in the bows. When *Cappelle* cants we haul on ropes to keep her level. Dogs bark and chase their tails. I push and pull. People get excited, a diver is sent for and someone cycles off to the Pet Shop for a sack of rabbit litter. (I find it peculiar that rabbits should enter the equation, but rabbit litter, if carefully spread by a diver, swells and will plug a leak as water pressure draws it in.) So, in the nick of time, *Cappelle* is hauled into deeper water and from thence to a berth, where we wait for the wood to "take up".

I thought I knew everything I need to know about jellyfish. In the Aegean I encountered the sinister Cyanea Capillata, which can inflict a severe sting. Families of them, gathering in the shade of the dinghy, took to pulsating beside *Cappelle*. When the Captain went over the side to wash the hull, I kept jelly watch in case of his urgent need to scramble out. I had also watched moon jellies floating in the sea currents. But what I never bargained for was the blood red horror we encountered in Ardfern. Beneath the surface of the water, like a gory hunk of raw meat, floated a potentially deadly jellyfish of a variety known as the Lion's Mane. It was all too easy for a swimmer, not realising such a creature lurked nearby, to swim through its toxic tentacles, which can stretch up to twenty feet or more. The sight of a jellyfish like this strengthened my resolve never to fall in again.

Another alien creature invades Holy Loch. Zanthoula reports seeing "weasels" leaping on and off yachts. Local people identify them as North American mink, which colonised after being released from fur farms by animal activists. When I see these musteline creatures, instinct tells me to be wary of confrontation. It is they who were responsible for the deaths of a family of cygnets that the parent birds blamed on a lone goose, which had lost its mate and followed them around. (Everyone calls it the "swoose" because it thinks it is a swan.) After the disappearance of the cygnets the cob and pen rushed at the innocent swoose and pecked it furiously. The mink are also guilty of terrorising the girls who sell ferry tickets on the pier by stealing their sandwiches.

With Felix, now joined by little sister Freya, we practise flying the cruising chute and "pinching" – sailing higher into the eye of the wind than close-hauled to slow us down, until the sails begin to luff – around Strone Point and in the Clyde basin where gannets give spectacular diving displays.

One day we sail for the upper Firth to visit the wreck of the Greek cargo ship, the MV *Captayannis,* known as "The Sugar Ship". I wonder whether, with a Greek Ship's Cat such as myself aboard, its situation could have been saved. But probably not. On a dark January night in

1974 the *Captayannis* and a BP tanker were anchored off waiting to enter the James Watt Dock to unload. But a gale blew up causing the Greek ship to drag her anchor towards the tanker, where the latter's tautened chain ripped through her hull. The ship's pumps could not cope and, although Captain Theodorakis Ionnis did his best to ground his ship on a sandbank, her hull profile made her unstable and she settled on her port side. All the souls were saved. But the cargo of sugar was lost to the sea. A haven for seabirds and fish, the *Captayannis* rests on the sandbank still.

Of course, it is my job to keep an eye on the two Fs – as if I haven't enough responsibility already. (Felix's forte is rowing the dinghy while Freya's is reading off the GPS.) As for mishaps, we experience two with the Fs aboard – not enough for Freya, who relishes misadventures. "Is it an emergency?" she enquires brightly, her eyes shining. The first occurs when, on bringing the boat in, we find our berth occupied. Directed into another, which proves undredged, we hit a sandbank so violently Steve is thrown overboard. We are then shouted at by an unamused skipper whose yacht we just miss as we reverse out, about being unable to handle our own boat. To think this could happen during my skippership. As you can imagine, I see red and have to be restrained. The second incident has even greater trouble potential. We are enjoying a spanking sail up river after encountering contrary winds around Toward Point when it transpires that the wire main halyard winch is only fastened to the new mast with cheap alloy screws. To our amazement the weighty metal object suddenly tears away, mid-river, from its fastenings to whistle skywards where it remains dangling over us like a lump hammer waiting to strike, leaving us punching home under engine, expecting it to descend on our heads at any moment.

It does not, but Freya is disappointed the adventure ended so tamely.

THIRTY-EIGHT

Tir-na-nOg

In which we research the Greeks.

We round the Mull of Kintyre.

We plan to discover the island of perpetual kittenhood.

After exploring the green isle of Bute in a spell of glorious weather, we set off to Tarbert Loch Fyne via the Kyles of Bute and the Burnt Islands: Big Island, Heather Island and Yellow Island (Eilean Buidhe). All water-going traffic must travel through the narrows between these islets, marked by four light buoys, two on each side. As we make our way along I find myself eyeball to eyeball with seals.

Despite *Cappelle* having the right of way, a two-tier floating cocktail bar driven by an oligarch with a cigar in his mouth and a lady friend, forces us brutally aside. I rack my brains for a suitable code cushion to aim at it, settling on the one marked "B" meaning "I am discharging explosives". It is a pity it is too far to throw.

On Argyll's secret coast in the Kyles we pick up a mooring buoy for the night at Tighnabruaich, departing after a leisurely breakfast for Ardamont Point and open water. It is the first of September, perfect weather, with enough breeze to fill the sails but not enough to hinder our appreciation of the scenery. On Arran to the south the summit of Goat Fell bites into the sky, its point as sharp as a shark's tooth. The sun is warm and the air fresh. (In the Aegean the air never quite matches the northern tingle.) Hove to, Zanthoula tape-records the sea's vibrato against the hull.

Entry to the picturesque fishing village of Tarbert Loch Fyne is not for the foolhardy. (A Ship's Cat like me is essential for skilled navigation of the islet which sits in the entrance like a bung in a bottle.) The name Tarbert, referring to the isthmus linking East Loch Tarbert to the West Loch on which the village is built, derives from an ancient word meaning "across-carrying". In ancient times boats were hauled overland to be relaunched the other side, thus taking the short route and avoiding the hard sail round the Mull.

Zanthoula, balancing on a wobbly pontoon in the lagoon that seriously threatens to bounce her off, has a problem tying the boat up and does it sitting down, which prompts the Captain to order her to, "Stand up for goodness sake." Another yachtswoman, going to her aid, ends up yelling hysterically for assistance to get her off. It is often the way with boats, tension the order of the day. As for myself, I remain above this sort of nonsense, as a Ship's Cat should, the calm at the centre of fuss, as it were. Anyway, when my Pets depart to gorge themselves on Loch Fyne scallops and samphire, they bring back mussels and choice olives.

Our verdict on Tarbert where Scottish, English and French yachts mingle is that it is as pretty as a party-wrapped present. A clinker-built, gaff-rigged boat with a red sail, reminiscent of an old Thames barge, circles gently, adding to a scene that has the quality of a Dutch painting. (Zanthoula promptly wants to live in Tarbert.)

We wonder why a canal has not been built across the Mull from Tarbert instead of Crinan, a far longer route, but discover why when we trail up, and then down the far side of the steep hill that divides East Loch from West Loch. My Pets reach the edge of the water after stumbling through boggy sedge while I jump from reed clump to reed clump. The Captain is certain he glimpsed a large high-sided boat with oars through the trees. But when we reach shore it has vanished. "I DID see it!" he insists, surprised. I heard tell of Magnus Barefoot, who, a thousand years ago, had his men shoulder his long-boat across the isthmus as part of the circumnavigation by which he annexed Kintyre. When I meet a red-bearded, hairy-kneed giant in the village striding along in a tartan kilt, I am sure it is Magnus, but he is wearing sensible sandals, so maybe it wasn't.

Zanthoula insists on pursuing an investigation on my behalf, which might just confirm there might be Scots in my blood and that I really could be related to the Wacky MacWacksters of Auchtermuchty. After reading about the discovery of a Greek coin in a garden in Tarbert in 1885, she goes to see the local historian, Mr Ian MacIntyre, to ask what he know of the story. He did know about the coin, which he said Tarbert would like returned for their own museum. Though there is no evidence of Greeks in the town, there is evidence of the Romans. He thinks the coin might have been dropped by a Roman soldier. When Zanthoula consults the Senior Curator at the Hunterian Museum he confirms that the museum still has the coin, a trade coin, an Athenian Tetradrachm of 460 BC. Although it could have been dropped by a Roman soldier, the curator believes it more likely to have fallen out of the pocket of some Victorian collector back from the Grand Tour.

The twitchy feeling I experienced about Magnus Barefoot increases. Can I have been a Ship's Cat on his Long Boat? I feel sure I was the one who cadged a shoulder-carry across the isthmus by hiding under a thwart. The Vikings always employed Ships' Cats on their Long Boats. (I have heard that mice nested in Magnus Barefoot's beard.)

The deep-water marina at Portavadie is popular. Built on the site of an industrial folly, an oil rig construction, it offers world-class facilities to visiting yachtsmen. At luncheon in the restaurant the chef is so good as to devise a delicious plate of *nouvelle cuisine féline* especially for me. Zanthoula, who, before our visit, had been told about the ladies' loos, also comes away happy.

We intend to explore further afield but with Force 9 imminent, return to the Holy Loch I have no wish to encounter Hurakan, the Mayan God, who gave the hurricane its name – although there were Aegean winds I wish I hadn't missed. The *"Tellysaválatos"*, the baldness wind that rips hair out by the roots, sounds interesting, and I would have loved to experience the "*Skylogyrisménatos*", the dog-rolling wind that sends dogs tumbling over and over in the streets. (Needless to say, we cats are better at staying on our feet.)

For the final fling of season we round the Mull of Kintyre, the Scottish Cape Malea. BUT WATCH THE TIDES. Since it stretches to within eleven miles of the coast of Antrim, it became famous as a landing place for Irish immigrants (among them the ancestors of Paul McCartney). In the eighteenth century the last known family of British cannibals, who feasted on unwary travellers – and probably their cats as well – inhabited this wild spot, where belief in the Evil Eye was recorded as late as the 1920s. Zanthoula wears her Evil Eye on her neck chain. I suspect she does it for pretty. But my Evil Eye is a badge of office, a talisman, a reminder, a reassurance, a bit like the silver button Davie Balfour turned in his pocket in *Kidnapped*.

We leave for the Mull of Kintyre on a gently dreich day to sail the Sound of Kilbrennan and anchor at the tiny island of Sanda just south of the Mull, whose rock arch and lighthouse has earned it the name of "The Ship". (In an old book it is described as "having a harbour for barques".) We need to round the Mull before the main tidal stream sets in. If we get our timing right, the sea will be a favourable fair to slack as we progress up the west coast. I ensure we leave Sanda just as the pink knot of the sun begins to tie off the dark. At first the water is choppy, but, after a great day's sail, we drop anchor on the island of Gigha. (Zanthoula wants to go back there when its flowers are out.) Then we settle *Cappelle* for winter in Holy Loch under the watchful eye of her band of devoted carers, "The Last of the Summer Wine" – a Welshman, a Scotsman and a German.

Zanthoula keeps her boat key on a key ring of moonbeam silver. On its fob is engraved, "WISH IT, DREAM IT, DO IT..." Well, we did wish it, we did dream it, we did do it...AND we'll do more. But now it's time for me to loll in the lavender bushes and fill in my yachting diary. If you are a feisty cat like me, there is no better profession than mine. Leave everything undone you ought to have done, do everything you ought not to do, and then GO TO SEA. Be a Ship's Cat. That's the ticket.

Lavender is my happiness flower. I breathe it as I plan new adventures and dream of islands as yet unvisited, far-flung St Kilda, Staffa with its melodious cave, Shetland, the Shiant Islands, Islay, Isle de Ré in France, so many places, anywhere, everywhere, waiting to be seen.

Afterwards I snooze. My throat throbs and I purr. My paws work by themselves, my claws moving in and out as though I were kneading dough. I am content! I think of other happiness smells – cat mint, wet gear hanging in the wet wardrobe, teak oil, olives in a cocktail dish, fresh caught small fry, wormy plastic filler, crumpled duvets, taramasalata, the Captain's old jeans, Tilley lamps and whisky-drizzled haggis...then I drift off humming, "What a wonderful world," until the music changes into "My Blue Heaven". This is followed by the Shipping Forecast – "Viking, Forties, Cromarty, Marlin Head, Fair Isle, Finisterre..." The names roll musically off the tongue.

"My ship has sails that are made of silk
Her decks are trimmed with gold"

One day the Captain and Zanthoula and I plan to discover Tir-na-nOg, the Hebridean island of perpetual kittenhood. Here we will settle with *Cappelle*, knowing she has given us the time of our lives: "Haec Olim Meminisse Juvabit" – "The day will come when it will gladden the heart to remember this."

Sometimes I dream of sailing with Artemis again. Loosely she ties the tip of my tail to the moon and a bunch of stars and we sail by their light astride her broomstick, eating caramel crème with runcible spoons. Zanthoula sees us. Maybe you do too?

o – o – O – o – o

Tir-na-nOg

Lavender's blue, dilly, dilly,
Lavender wine
I'm her Ship's Cat and we get along fine
(Just so long as it's clear I'm not hers
But she's mine.)

The nose of Zanthoula is deep in a book
Laying it down,
She looks into my eyes.
"Dear Wacky, I'd lend you this diary to ponder
But think you have read it!"
she confides with a smile.

"Don't be silly!" I say, as I purr in reply:

"I wrote it."

December 2015